Mexican Expressions
❧ The Spice of a People ❧

Expresiones mexicanas
❧ El sabor de un pueblo ❧

Mexican Expressions

❧ The Spice of a People ❧

Expresiones mexicanas

❧ El sabor de un pueblo ❧

Octavio A. Ballesteros, Ed. D.
and
María del Carmen Ballesteros, M. Ed.

EAKIN PRESS ❧ Austin, Texas

For CIP
information,
please access:
www.loc.gov

FIRST EDITION
Copyright © 2002
By Octavio A. Ballesteros and María del Carmen
Ballesteros
Published in the United States of America
By Eakin Press
A Division of Sunbelt Media, Inc.
P.O. Drawer 90159 ☐ Austin, Texas 78709-0159
email: sales@eakinpress.com
☐ website: www.eakinpress.com ☐
ALL RIGHTS RESERVED.
1 2 3 4 5 6 7 8 9
1-57168-575-8

To the late Glodomiro E. González. May his love for
the Mexican culture and the Spanish language
long be remembered by his relatives and
friends who live on both sides of
the Texas-Mexico border.
His friendliness and
wit will not be
forgotten.

Contents / Índice

Preface

An expression may be defined as a word, phrase, or statement that is characteristic of a particular language and culture. Expressions are used to add humor to a conversation, prove a philosophical point, advise a family member, describe a situation, or depict a human condition.

Many expressions are idioms. An idiom is an expression of a particular language that is unique to that language grammatically. The true meaning of an idiomatic expression usually cannot be determined by analyzing its component parts.

Idioms often create a picture in the mind of both the speaker and the listener. The student of idiomatic expressions is keenly aware that many idioms contain both imagery and impact. When an idiomatic expression is uttered, it tends to produce an image in the listener's mind which often creates a strong impact or effect on the listener. An example of an idiomatic expression which tends to create an image in the mind of the listener is: *"Echaron la casa por la ventana."* (See Expression 295 for the English translation.)

Some expressions are figures of speech that tend to use words in an unusual sense to add flavor to a statement or conversation. Examples of figures of speech are metaphors and similes.

In this Spanish-English bilingual collection, the reader will find ample examples of metaphors and similes. An example of a metaphor in this anthology is: *"El mundo es un pañuelo"* (see Expression 129). An example of a simile in this anthology is: *"Tiene ojos de chivo empachado"* (see Expression 400).

Though this volume is filled with expressions that contain unique and descriptive figures of speech, the author and coauthor each have a favorite expression. The author's favorite expression is: *"Entró como burro sin mecate"* (see Expression 86). The coauthor's favorite expression is: *"¿Cedacito nuevo, dónde te pondré?"* (see Expression 264).

Most of the expressions are written in sentence form which we believe will facilitate language learning on the part of the reader who wants to increase his Spanish proficiency. The reader who masters the meaning of each expression contained herein will be well along the road to learning the Spanish language and understanding the Mexican mind. It should be pointed out that persons unfamiliar with the Spanish language as spoken in the New World may experience some difficulty in determining the full or exact meaning of those expressions, which are figurative in nature. For this reason, each expression has been carefully translated from Spanish to English. Each expression has been translated literally. When the literal English translation did not transmit the original meaning of the Mexican expression, the expression also was paraphrased. In some cases, Mexican expressions were paired with their American counterparts. The purpose of the pairing was to show the similarities and differences between the expressions of the two cultural groups. The overall aim was to present the literal and actual meaning of each expression.

One objective of *Mexican Expressions* is to offer the reader an uncommon collection of frequently used idioms and literal Spanish expressions that are heard in the daily speech of native Spanish speakers in Mexico and Texas. The authors believe that this volume fills a void in Mexican American literature. To our knowledge, no comparable bilingual book of Mexican expressions exists.

A second objective of the book is to produce a work that can be used as a supplementary reader in Spanish language courses. Though a book of Mexican expressions cannot replace a Spanish textbook, a book of expressions can add color, variety, and character to the Spanish language structures that students learn from a basic textbook.

A third objective of *Mexican Expressions* is to provide the reader with a deeper understanding of the Spanish language spoken by

Mexicans and some Mexican Americans. Actually, this collection is intended for anyone who wants to learn more about Spanish, the Mexican culture, and the Hispanic mind. Puerto Ricans, Central Americans, Cuban Americans, South Americans, and Spanish Americans probably will enjoy reading these Mexican expressions, because these groups share a common culture—the Hispanic culture, which originated in Spain. An example of an expression that undoubtedly originated in Spain is: "*No hay moros en la costa*" (see Expression 550). This expression goes back to the days when Spain was concerned with expelling the *moros* (Moors) from its territory.

On the other hand, it is unlikely that anyone will dispute that Expression 92 ("*Guajolote que se sale del huacal termina en mole*") originated in Mexico. This expression is definitely Mexican in origin because *guajolote, huacal,* and *mole* are three terms that are distinctively Mexican.

The expressions in this compilation are listed under twenty-one categories of social interaction. Each expression has been assigned a number, which appears above the expression.

This collection grew from the authors' longstanding interest in the idioms and other expressions that they heard in conversations in Mexico and various parts of Texas. (The authors are frequent travelers to Mexico.)

The compilers believe that the expressions of a people are demonstrations of their culture's spirit, personality, behavior, and social values. Expressions also contain the hopes, frustrations, and ambitions of a cultural group. There is no doubt that cultural bonding occurs when Mexicans exchange expressions in a conversation.

When one captures a verbal expression on paper, one captures part of the culture from which the expression emanates. The compilers believe that this collection of expressions captures the spice and essence of the Mexican culture and the Spanish language as spoken in Mexico and Texas. Once the reader has read this collection, we feel that the reader will agree that expressions truly add savor to a Mexican's daily conversation.

The vast majority of the expressions in this work are written in informal language, the manner in which expressions are spoken by the general population of Mexico and Mexican Americans in Texas. The expressions are not written in the King's Spanish because most Mexican expressions are spoken in the language of the people. Still, the expressions are written in a solid linguistic form.

It took the compilers more than ten years to collect the expressions contained herein. The collection process was a slow one, because the authors decided that each expression had to be contributed to them by a Mexican citizen or a Mexican American. Most of the contributors were from northern Mexico and South Texas, while some contributors were from central Mexico and Houston, Texas.

This collection of expressions was obtained primarily from interviews and conversations with older Hispanics. Some expressions were acquired from conversations with relatives, friends, and acquaintances. A few expressions were procured from Mexican soap operas, Mexican motion pictures, and television personalities who injected Mexican expressions into their conversations.

Lastly, some expressions were acquired at various social gatherings. Without question, some of the the most memorable expressions were heard at gatherings.

One method of obtaining expressions from individuals was to orally provide them with one or two expressions. In many instances, the individual would smile or nod his head, comment on the expression, and then provide the authors with an expression that was dear to his heart.

Those expressions which aroused the sensibilities of the compilers were recorded on index cards in Spanish. At a later time, the expressions were translated into English.

Not all of the expressions collected by the authors are included in this volume, because we decided to limit this collection to no more than 620 expressions. (The actual number of expressions in this work is 618.) The expressions not included in this collection hopefully will appear in a subsequent volume.

There are countless Mexican expressions that still need to be located, captured, recorded, and published in book form. The authors are still gathering those elusive expressions, which sometimes seem to be hiding from us. It is unlikely that we will succeed in finding that "last slippery expression" that we know is out there *somewhere*. However, if we persevere, perhaps one day we can hold our heads high knowing that we have found the "best of the best" Mexican expressions. But truthfully, that "*es el cuento de nunca acabar*" (see Expression 509).

Because Mexican expressions are found in the minds of Mexicans and Mexican Americans, the authors needed assistance in locating, selecting, and interpreting some of the idioms that appear in this collection. The authors gratefully acknowledge the generous support provided to them by the following persons: María B. Gonzales, Aurora G. Rodríguez, Emma G. Cavazos, María Elena Palacios, Rebecca G. Sermino, and Ernesto Rodríguez.

Octavio A. Ballesteros
María del Carmen Ballesteros
San Antonio, Texas

Prefacio

Una expresión se puede definir como una palabra, frase, o declaración que es característica de un idioma y una cultura particular. Las expresiones se usan para añadir humor a una conversación, justificar un punto filosófico, aconsejar a un miembro de la familia, describir una situación, o representar una condición humana.

Muchas expresiones son modismos. Un modismo es una expresión de una lengua particular que es única gramaticalmente a esa lengua. El significado verdadero de un modismo generalmente no se puede determinar analizando sus partes componentes.

Los modismos muchas veces producen una imagen en la mente de la persona que está hablando, así como en la del que está escuchando. El estudiante de modismos está agudamente consciente que muchos modismos producen un conjunto de imagenes y causan un impacto. Cuando un modismo es expresado, el modismo tiene la tendencia de producir una imagen en la mente del escuchante que con frecuencia le ocasiona un impacto o efecto fuerte. Un ejemplo de un modismo que tiende causar una imagen en la mente del escuchante es: "Echaron la casa por la ventana" (véase la expresión 295 para la tradución al inglés).

Algunas expresiones son figuras gramaticales que tienen la tendencia de usar palabras en un sentido raro para agregarle sabor al relato o conversación. Algunos ejemplos de figuras gramaticales son las metáforas y las símiles.

En esta colección bilingüe de inglés y español, el lector encontrará bastantes ejemplos de metáforas y símiles. Un ejemplo de una metáfora en esta antología es: "El mundo es un pañuelo" (véase la expresión 129). Un ejemplo de un símil en esta antología es: "Tiene ojos de chivo empachado" (véase la expresión 400).

Aunque este tomo está lleno de expresiones que contienen figuras gramaticales raras y descriptivas, cada uno de los colaboradores tiene su expresión favorita. La expresión favorita del primer autor es: "Entró como burro sin mecate" (véase la expresión 86). La expresión favorita del segundo autor es: "¿Cedacito nuevo dónde te pondré?" (véase la expresión 264).

La mayoría de las expresiónes están escritas en forma de oración. Nuestra intención es de facilitar el estudio del lenguaje en el lector que desee aumentar su pericia en español. El lector que domine el significado de cada expresión de este libro se encontrará bien encarrilado hacia el aprendizaje del lenguaje español y hacia el pensamiento mexicano. Tal vez las personas que no conocen el idioma español como el que se habla en el Nuevo Mundo puedan tener dificultad en determinar el significado completo o exacto de esas expresiones que son de tipo figurativo. Por ese motivo, cada expresión ha sido cuidadosamente traducida del español al inglés. Cada expresión ha sido literalmente traducida. Cuando la tradución literal al inglés no logró transmitir el sentido original de la expresión mexicana, la expresión también fue parafraseada. En ciertas situaciones, las expresiones fueron pareadas con sus contrapartes americanas. La intención de parear las expresiones fue para mostrar la semejanza de dos grupos culturales. El objetivo fue para presentar el sentido literal y actual de cada expresión.

Un objetivo de *Mexican Expressions* es de ofrecer al lector una colección extraordinaria en español literal de expresiones y modismos que son usadas con frecuencia en las conversaciones diarias de los nativos hispanos en México y Texas. Los autores piensan que este tomo llena un vacio en la literatura mexicoamericana. Para nuestro conocimiento, no existe otro libro bilingüe comparable de expresiones mexicanas.

Un objetivo secundario de este libro es de producir una obra que se pueda usar como libro de lectura suplemental en cursos de español. Aun cuando un libro de expresiones mexicanas no pueda reemplazar un libro de texto de español, un libro de expresiones puede agregarle color, variedad, y carácter a las estructuras del idioma español que los estudiantes aprenden de un libro de texto básico.

Un tercer objetivo de *Mexican Expressions* es de proporcionar al lector un entendimiento más profundo del lenguaje español que es hablado por mexicanos y mexicoamericanos: De hecho, esta colección es para toda persona que desee aprender más acerca del idioma español, la cultura mexicana, y la mente hispana. Los puertorriqueños, los centroamericanos, los cubanoamericanos, los sudamericanos, y los hispanoamericanos probablemente gozarán leyendo estas expresiones mexicanas, porque cada uno de los grupos mencionados comparten una cultura común—la cultura hispana que originó en Eepaña. Una expresión que indudablemente originó en España es: "No hay moros en la costa" (véase la expresión 550). Esta expresión es de los días cuando España estaba preocupada por expulsar los moros de su territorio.

Por otra parte, es muy improbable que alguien vaya a disputar que la expresión 92 ("Guajolote que se sale del huacal termina en mole") originó en México. Esta expresión es definitivamente mexicana porque *guajolote, huacal,* y *mole* son tres palabras que son distintamente mexicanas.

Las expresiones en esta compilación están anotadas en una lista de veintiuna categorias de actividades sociales. Cada expresión ha sido asignada un número, el cual aparece sobre la expresión.

Esta colección fue aumentando por el interés de larga duración por parte de los autores hacia los modismos y otras expresiones que escucharon en conversaciones en México y en varios lugares de Texas. (Los autores viajean con mucha frecuencia a México.)

Los compiladores creen que las expresiones de un pueblo son demostraciones del espíritu, de la personalidad, del comportamiento, y de los méritos sociales de su cultura. Las expresiónes también contienen las esperanzas, frustaciones, y aspiraciones de un grupo cultural. No hay ninguna duda que una unión cultural sucede cuando los mexicanos intercambían expresiónes en una conversación.

Cuando uno captura una expresión verbal por escrito, uno captura parte de la cultura de donde la expresión brotó. Los compiladores creen que esta colección de expresiones captura el sabor y la esencia de la cultura mexicana y del idioma español como es hablado en México y Texas. Nosotros opinamos que una vez que el lector haya leído esta colección, él estará de acuerdo que las expresiones verdaderamente añaden sabor a la conversación diaria de un mexicano.

La mayoría de las expresiónes de esta obra están escritas informalmente porque esa es la manera que las expresiones son habladas por la población general de México y por los mexicoamericanos en Texas. Las expresiones no están escritas en el español del rey y su corte real porque la mayoría de las expresiones mexicanas son habladas en el lenguaje del pueblo. A pesar de eso, las expresiones están escritas en una forma lingüística solida.

Les tomó más de diez años a los compiladores para coleccionar las expresiones que se encuentran en esta obra. El proceso de coleccionar fue muy lento, porque los autores determinaron que cada una de las expresiones que les contribuyeron tenía que venir de un ciudadano mexicano o mexicoamericano. La mayor parte de los contribuyentes fueron del norte de México y del sur de Texas mientras algunos contribuyentes fueron del interior de México y de Houston, Texas.

Esta colección de expresiones fue obtenida principalmente de entrevistas y conversaciones con hispanos mayores. Algunas expresiones fueron adquiridas de conversaciones con parientes, amigos, y conocidos. Otras fueron obtenidas de telenovelas mexicanas, cine mexicano, y personajes de la televisión quienes inyectaron expresiones mexicanas en sus conversaciones.

Finalmente, algunas expresiones fueron adquiridas en varias reuniones sociales. Sin duda, algunas de las expresiones más memorables fueron escuchadas en reuniones.

Un método que usaron los autores para obtener expresiónes de individuos fue de verbalmente proporcionarlos con una o dos expresiones. En muchos casos, el individuo se sonreía o hacía un movimiento con la cabeza, hacía un comentario acerca de la expresión, pero después les proporcionaba a los autores una expresión muy querida para él.

Aquellas expresiones que despertaron las sensibilidades de los compiladores fueron anotadas en una tarjetita índice. Después las expresiones fueron traducidas al inglés.

No todas las expresiones que los autores colectaron están incluidas en este tomo, porque decidimos limitar esta colección a no más de 620 expresiones. (El número verdadero de expresiónes en esta colección es 618.) Las expresiones que no están incluidas en esta colección esperamos que aparezcan en un tomo subsecuente.

Hay innumerables expresiones que todavía necesitan ser localizadas, capturadas, apuntadas, y publicadas en forma de libro. Los autores todavía están juntando aquellas expresiones ilusivas que algunas veces parece que se están escondiendo de nosotros. Es improbable que vamos a lograr encontrar aquella "última expresión resbaladiza" que nosotros sabemos está allá en algún lugar. Sin embargo, si persistimos, tal vez algun día podamos ver hacia arriba sabiendo que hemos encontrado "lo mejor de lo mejor" en expresiones mexicanas. Pero verdaderamente eso "es el cuento de nunca acabar" (véase la expresión 509).

Por la razón de que las expresiones mexicanas se encuentran el las mentes de mexicanos y mexicoamericanos, los autores necesitaron asistencia en localizar, seleccionar, e interpretar algunos de los modismos que aparecen en esta colección. Los autores agradecidamente reconocen el generoso apoyo que les fue proporcionado por las siguientes personas: María B. Gonzales, Aurora G. Rodríguez, Emma G. Cavazos, María Elena Palacios, Rebecca G. Sermino, y Ernesto Rodríguez.

Octavio A. Ballesteros
María del Carmen Ballesteros
San Antonio, Texas

Suggested Ways to Use This Book

The expressions in this collection can be used to learn more about Mexico, Mexicans, Mexican Americans, and the Spanish language.

Middle school, high school, and college students who are studying Spanish can use the expressions in this book to gain insights into the Hispanic culture.

Mexican Expressions is a Spanish-English bilingual book that can be used by English speakers who want to learn Spanish and by Spanish speakers who want to learn English.

This book can be given as a gift to a Hispanic friend who enjoys reading books written in the Spanish language.

This bilingual anthology of Mexican expressions should prove useful to anyone who derives pleasure from reading the humorous, wise, descriptive, and moralistic statements found in many of the expressions of Mexico.

Teachers of bilingual students can use the expressions in this book to stimulate creative writing in their students.

Persons who enjoyed reading *Mexican Sayings* and *Mexican Proverbs* (both by the same author) also will profit from reading *Mexican Expressions,* because the three books contain related material.

Sugerencias acerca del uso de este libro

Las expresiones en esta colección se pueden usar para aprender más acerca de México, los mexicoamericanos, y el idioma español.

Estudiantes de la escuela intermedia o secundaria, asi como estudiantes de la universidad que están estudiando español, pueden usar estas expresiones para obtener un conocimiento más profundo acerca de la cultura hispana.

Mexican Expressions es un libro bilingüe en español e inglés que puede ser utilizado por personas que hablan inglés que deseen aprender español y por personas que hablan español que deseen aprender inglés.

Este libro puede ser obsequiado como un regalo a un amigo hispano que goza leyendo libros escritos en el idioma español.

Esta antología bilingüe de expresiones mexicanas mostrará ser útil para toda persona que obtiene placer leyendo las declaraciones humorísticas, juiciosas, descriptivas, y morales que se encuentran en muchas de las expresiones de México.

Maestros de estudiantes bilingües pueden usar las expresiones en este libro para estimular escritura creativa en sus alumnos.

Las personas que disfrutaron de haber leído *Mexican Sayings* y *Mexican Proverbs* (ambos por el mismo autor) también aprovecharan leyendo *Mexican Expressions* porque los tres libros contienen material relacionado.

Expresiones humorísticas
Humorous Expressions

☙ 1 ❧

A los pobres y a los feos todo se les va en deseos.
The poor and the homely spend all of their time wishing.

☙ 2 ❧

Al mal músico hasta las uñas le estorban.
a. To the bad musician, even the fingernails hinder him.
b. The incompetent worker is always making excuses.

☙ 3 ❧

Anda a pie.
He is on foot. (Said humorously of a person who owns an expensive car.)

☙ 4 ❧

Anda en asuntos de faldas.
a. He is on affairs of the skirts.
b. He is chasing skirts.

≈ 5 ≈

Apúntalo en el hielo.
   a. Write it down on ice.
   b. Please record my tab (bill) on ice.

≈ 6 ≈

Atácate Matías que de esto no hay todos los días.
   a. Stuff yourself, Matthias, because we do not have this
      every day.
   b. Eat heartily, because we do not eat this type of food
      every day.

≈ 7 ≈

A todo se acostumbra el cuerpo menos a no comer.
   The body can become accustomed to anything except to
      not eating.

≈ 8 ≈

Como le gusta mover la sin hueso.
   a. How he likes to move the one without a bone.
   b. How he likes to move his tongue.
   c. He loves to talk.

≈ 9 ≈

Con amor y aguardiente nada se siente.
   a. With love and brandy, nothing is felt.
   b. You feel no pain under the influence of love and brandy.

≈ 10 ≈

Con curas y gatos pocos tratos.
   a. With priests and cats, few deals.
   b. Make few agreements with priests and cats.

2

Con mucho gusto y nada de ganas.
    a. With all pleasure and no desire.
    b. I'll be happy to do it, though I really don't feel like doing it.

Cuando la limosna es grande, hasta el santo desconfía.
    When the alms are excessive, even the saint becomes suspicious.

Cuando se vayan, apagen la luz.
    a. When you leave, turn out the light.
    b. I'm going to bed. Please turn out the lights when you
       leave.

Dado y rempujado.
    a. Given and pushed.
    b. Give them an inch and they will take a foot.

De pura lástima te abrazan y quieres que te aprieten.
    From pure pity they embrace you, and you (also) want them
       to squeeze you.

Donde no hay trancazos, no hay abrazos.
    Where there are no blows, there are no embraces.

El diablo no es tan diablo.
    a. The devil isn't such a devil.
    b. The devil isn't as bad as most people believe.

≫ 18 ≪

El que cambia de baraja o de mujer, mejor suerte quiere tener.
He who changes his playing cards or his woman does so to
improve his luck.

≫ 19 ≪

El que ha nacido en petate siempre anda oliendo a tule.
The person who was born on a mat always smells like straw.

≫ 20 ≪

El que nace para payaso, del cielo le caen las pinturas.
For the person who was born to be a clown, the face paint
falls from the sky.

≫ 21 ≪

El que se junta conmigo ni en la casa lo regañan.
a. The person who associates with me not even in his home is
scolded.
b. If you associate with me, your wife will not scold you when
you get home.

≫ 22 ≪

Enfermo que come, no muere.
The patient who eats will not die.

≫ 23 ≪

Enfermo que come y bebe, el diablo que se lo crea.
a. The sick person who eats and drinks, let the devil believe
him.
b. The person who eats and drinks, let the devil believe he is
sick, because I don't.
c. The sick person who eats and drinks is not really sick.

≈ 24 ≈

En tierra de los mudos el tartamudo es rey.
In the land of the mute, the stutterer is king.

≈ 25 ≈

Eso pasó cuando Adán vendía helotes.
a. That happened when Adam sold corn.
b. That occurred ages ago.

≈ 26 ≈

Está en todo menos en misa.
a. He/she is into everything except mass.
b. He/she can be found doing everything except going to church.

≈ 27 ≈

Está pelón y quiere que le hagan trenzas.
He's bald and he wants them to braid his hair.

≈ 28 ≈

Es tonto pero no tanto.
a. He is foolish, but not so much.
b. He is foolish, but not too foolish.

≈ 29 ≈

Estudió para papa y salió camote.
He studied to be Pope/potato and became a sweet potato.
(Note: The Spanish word *papa* means both "Pope" and "potato." This expression is a play on the word *potato,* and is a humorous way of saying that a person didn't achieve his vocational potential.)

≈ 30 ≈

Es una bruja clásica; nomás le falta la escoba.
She is a classic witch; all she lacks is a broom.

Fue mesero en la santa cena.
    a. He was a waiter at the Last Supper.
    b. He has been around for years.

Fuí por lana y volví trasquilado.
    a. I went for wool and I returned sheared.
    b. I went to obtain money, and I returned fleeced.

Gracias por la flor; mañana vuelvo por la maceta.
    a. Thank you for the flower; tomorrow I will return for the
       flower pot.
    b. Thanks for the compliment; tomorrow I will return for a
       bigger compliment.

Hijo de tu hija es tu nieto; hijo de tu hijo, quien sabe.
    The son of your daughter is your grandson; the son of your
       son, who knows.

Juan Gómez lo trae y Juan Gómez se lo come.
    a. Juan Gómez brings it and Juan Gómez eats it.
    b. I brought it to the party, and I'm going to eat it.

La carne de marrano no es transparente.
    a. Pig meat is not transparent.
    b. His carcass is blocking my view.

❧ 37 ❧

Le falta un tornillo.
  a. He lacks a screw.
  b. He has a screw missing.
  c. He's not all there.

❧ 38 ❧

Le patina el coco.
  a. His coconut skates.
  b. His head (mind) isn't all there.
  c. He has a screw missing.

❧ 39 ❧

Me dicen el pichón porque siempre me despluman.
  a. They call me the pigeon because they always pluck me.
  b. They call me a pigeon because people always take advantage of me.

❧ 40 ❧

Me duele la bola—la bola de años que tengo.
  a. The ball hurts me—the ball of years that I have.
  b. I am suffering from "ball-itis"—the ball of years that I have lived.

❧ 41 ❧

Me vieron la "p" en la frente. (Note: The letter "p" stands for the Spanish word *pendejo*. A *pendejo* is a coward or a fool.)
  a. They saw a "p" on my forehead.
  b. They saw the letter "p" on my forehead.
  c. They saw the word "fool" on my forehead.
  d. They took me for a fool.

❧ 42 ❧

Mucho ruido y pocas nueces.
   a. Much noise and few nuts.
   b. I hear much noise, but I see few nuts falling from the tree.
   c. There is much smoke but little fire.

❧ 43 ❧

Nada más para la muela picada.
   a. Nothing more than for the pricked tooth.
   b. They gave me only enough to fill a tooth cavity.
   c. They gave me only a small amount.

❧ 44 ❧

No es miedo, es precaución.
   a. It's not fear, it's precaution.
   b. I'm not afraid; I'm just trying to protect myself against harm.

❧ 45 ❧

Nomás le falta el resplandor.
   a. He only lacks the brightness.
   b. He only needs a halo.
   c. He's so good that all he needs is a halo.

❧ 46 ❧

Lo único que le falta es el molcajete.
   a. The only thing she lacks is a molcajete. (A molcajete is a
      stone mortar and pestle.)
   b. She has everything but the kitchen sink.

Lo único que le falta es el molcajete.

❧ 47 ❧

Parece calzón sin gente.
   a. He resembles trousers without a person.
   b. He resembles a pair of trousers without a person inside of
      them.
   c. He's nothing but skin and bone.

❧ 48 ❧

Para que no digan que vine de violín.
   a. So that they don't say that I came as a fiddler.
   b. I brought something to the party so that they don't say
      that I came empty-handed.

❧ 49 ❧

Pasó a panzasos.
   a. He passed by pushes from the belly.
   b. He passed by pushing with his belly.
   c. He passed by the skin of his teeth.

❧ 50 ❧

¿Patas, pa' qué son?
   a. Feet, for what are you?
   b. Feet, why do I have you?
   c. Feet, get me out of here.

❧ 51 ❧

Peor es nada, dijo el calvo cuando se hayó un pelo.
   a. Worse is nothing, said the bald man when he found a hair.
   b. It's better than nothing, said the bald man when he found
      a hair on his head.

Piensa que es la última soda en el desierto.
   a. He thinks he is the last soda (soft drink) in the desert.
   b. He's stuck on himself.

Planchó el asiento.
   a. She smoothed (ironed) the seat.
   b. She smoothed the seat at the dance.
   c. She was a wallflower at the dance.

Poquito porque es bendito.
   a. Very little because it is blessed.
   b. I am going to give you only a small amount because it is
      blessed.

Por ponerle Pancha Ramos, le pusimos "la fregamos."
   a. For putting her 'Pancha Ramos,' we put her 'washed.'
   b. For naming her Pancha Ramos, we ruined her.
   c. We should have given her a better name.

Primero con agua, después, sin agua, y al último como aqua.
   a. At first with water, then without water, and ultimately like
      water.
   b. At first you drink liquor with water, then you drink liquor
      without water, and finally you drink liquor like water.

¿Qué comes que advinas?
   a. What do you eat that allows you to foretell events?
   b. What qualifies you to prophesy?

❧ 58 ❧

Que Dios se lo pague porque yo no.
May God repay you, because I won't.

❧ 59 ❧

Salió de Guatemala y entró a Guatepeor.
a. He left Guatemala and entered Guatepeor.
b. He went from bad to worse.
(Note: Though Guate*mala* is a Central American nation, Guate*peor* is a nonexistent place. This epxression is a humorous way of saying that a person went from a bad [*mala*] situation to a worse [*peor*] one.)

❧ 60 ❧

Se cree la mamá de Tarzán.
a. She thinks she's Tarzan's mother.
b. She has a high opinion of herself.

❧ 61 ❧

Si están enterando gratis, hay que morirse.
a. If they are burying free of charge, one should die.
b. A person should take advantage of free burials.
c. One should take advantage of things that are free.

❧ 62 ❧

Si tomas para olvidar, paga antes de empezar.
If you drink to forget, pay before you begin.

❧ 63 ❧

Te roban los calcetines sin quitarte los zapatos.
a. They steal your socks without taking off your shoes.
b. They are so crafty that they can steal your socks without taking off your shoes.

Ve a ver si ya puso la marrana.

❧ 64 ❧

Todos los días nace un tonto. Hay que buscarlo.
Every day a fool is born. One must find him.

❧ 65 ❧

Unos vivos y otros tontos, pero todos comen.
    a. Some are clever and some are foolish, but they all eat.
    b. Clever or foolish, they eat three times a day.

❧ 66 ❧

Ve a ver si ya puso la marrana.
    a. Go see if the pig has laid eggs.
    b. Go see if the impossible has happened.
    c. Make yourself scarce.

≈ 67 ≈

Voy a colgar los guantes.
    a. I am going to hang up my gloves.
    b. I am going to retire.

≈ 68 ≈

Ya comí, ya me voy.
    a. Now I have eaten, now I go.
    b. Now that I have eaten your food, I will leave.

≈ 69 ≈

¿Ya lo bailado, quién me lo quita?
    a. That which has been danced (taken), who can take it away?
    b. Who can take it from me once it is in my possession?

≈ 70 ≈

Ya me casé, ya me amolé.
    a. Now I have married, now I am ruined.
    b. Now that I have married, I am devastated.

Expresiones acerca de animales

Expressions About Animals

∽ 71 ∾

A cada pájaro le gusta su nido.
  a. Each bird likes his nest.
  b. A man's home is his castle.

∽ 72 ∾

Algún día comerá mi gato sardina. (humorístico)
  a. Someday my cat will eat sardines. (humorous)
  b. Someday my ship will come in.

∽ 73 ∾

Al mejor casador se le escapa la liebre.
  a. The hare escapes from the best hunter.
  b. The best hunter can fail to bag the rabbit.

∽ 74 ∾

A lo rojo se le va un toro.
  a. To the red goes the bull.
  b. A bull is attracted to red.
  c. The color red draws attention.

❧ 75 ❧

Al perro flaco se le cargan las pulgas.
The skinny dog is the one that gets loaded with fleas.

❧ 76 ❧

Anda como gallina clueca.
a. She is going around like a brooding hen.
b. She is as excited as a brooding hen.

❧ 77 ❧

Andan como auras viejas.
a. They are going around like old vultures.
b. They are waiting for an opportunity to pounce (on a person or situation).

❧ 78 ❧

A otro perro con ese hueso.
a. To another dog with that bone.
b. Take that bone to another dog.
c. Tell that story to another person.
d. I don't believe that tale.

❧ 79 ❧

Aquí hay gato encerrado.
a. Here there is a locked-up cat.
b. I smell a confined cat.
c. I smell a rat.

❧ 80 ❧

Caballo que vuela no quiere espuela.
a. The horse that flies does not want the spur.
b. The fast horse does not have to be spurred.

Cada perico a su estaca.

❧ 81 ❧

Cada perico a su estaca.
    a. Each parrot to his stick.
    b. Each person to his position.

❧ 82 ❧

Cuando la perra es brava, hasta los de casa muerde.
    a. When the female dog is ferocious, it bites even the members of the household.
    b. Some ferocious dogs will even bite the hand that feeds them.

❧ 83 ❧

Dando dando, pajarito cantando.
    a. Giving, giving, little bird singing.
    b. I did my part, so compensate me.
    c. Tit for tat.

❧ 84 ❧

El caballo del patrón nomás el patrón lo monta.
The horse of the master, only the master mounts.

❧ 85 ❧

En menos que canta un gallo.
   a. In less time than a rooster can sing (crow).
   b. It happened quickly.

❧ 86 ❧

Entró como burro sin mecate.
   a. He came in like a donkey without a rope.
   b. He entered the room like an unrestrained donkey.

❧ 87 ❧

Eres más terco que una mula.
   You are more stubborn than a mule.

❧ 88 ❧

Esa clase de pulga no brinca en tu petate.
   a. That sort of flea does not jump on your mat.
   b. That person is out of your reach.

❧ 89 ❧

Es como llevar peces al mar.
   a. It is like taking fish to the sea.
   b. There is no need for you to do that.
   c. That's like selling ice to the Eskimos.

❧ 90 ❧

Es como quitarle un pelo a un oso.
   a. It's like taking a hair from a bear.
   b. That's no easy task.

❧ 91 ❧

Es más vivo que un coyote.
   a. He's more clever than a coyote.
   b. He's as sly as a fox.

Guajolote que se sale del huacal termina en mole.
  a. The turkey that gets out of the crate ends as turkey with gravy.
  b. The turkey that escapes from the crate ends up on someone's plate.

Hay tantas yeguas y yo que ni un burro tengo. (humorístico)
  a. There are so many mares, and I don't even have a donkey. (humorous)
  b. There are so many horses around here, and I don't even have a donkey.
  c. There are so many beautiful women, and I don't even have a hag.

Hijo de gato casa ratón.
  a. The son of a cat hunts mice.
  b. Like father, like son.

Lo traen como perro en barrio ajeno.
  a. They have him like a dog in a strange neighborhood.
  b. They are treating him like the new dog/kid on the block.

Me dejaron como palo de perico. (humorístico)
  a. They left me like a parrot's perch.
  b. They left me messed up.

Me tumbó la burra.
a. The female donkey knocked me down.
b. She replaced me.
c. She took my place.

¡No puede ver caballo ensillado!
a. He cannot see a saddled horse!
b. He cannot walk past a saddled horse.
c. If he sees a saddled horse, he has to ride it.
d. If he sees an opportunity, he takes it.

No seas pájaro de mal agüero.
a. Do not be a bird of bad omen.
b. Do not be a bearer of bad news.

No se paran ni las moscas.
a. Not even the flies stop.
b. Not even the flies come to visit.
c. Business is slow.

No te metas en las patas de los caballos.
a. Do not get in between the horse's feet.
b. Don't get tangled in a mess.
c. Stay out of trouble.

No vayas a pisar un sapo.
a. Don't step on a frog.
b. Since you slept so late, be careful not to step on a frog.

∽ 103 ∾

Otra vez la burra al maíz.
   a. Again the female donkey to the corn.
   b. Again the donkey heads for the corn.
   c. It happened again.

∽ 104 ∾

Otro gallo nos cantará.
   a. Another rooster will sing to us.
   b. Things will get better.

∽ 105 ∾

Por un borrego no se juzga la manada.
   You do not judge the flock by one sheep.

∽ 106 ∾

¿Qué mosca te picó?
   a. What fly bit you?
   b. What's bothering you?

∽ 107 ∾

Que susto llevaron las gallinas.
   a. What a scare the chickens had.
   b. We received a terrible scare.

∽ 108 ∾

Se acabó la gallina de los huevos de oro.
   a. The end has come to the hen that laid the golden eggs.
   b. The source of the wealth/money has died.
   c. They killed the goose that laid the golden eggs.

Se acostó con las gallinas.
   a. He went to bed with the chickens.
   b. He went to bed very early.

Se le dormió el gallo. (humorístico)
   a. The rooster went to sleep on him. (humorous)
   b. He awaked late because his rooster did not crow in the morning.
   c. He missed an opportunity.

Tantos perros con un pobre hueso.
   a. So many dogs with one poor bone.
   b. Too many dogs are chewing on that small bone.
   c. There are too many workers on that project.

Tenemos que agarrar el toro por los cuernos.
   We have to grab the bull by the horns.

Tiene más vidas que un gato.
   He has more lives than a cat.

Vete a echar pulgas a otra parte.
   a. Go and cast fleas someplace else.
   b. Go bother someone else.

Expresiones filosóficas
Philosophical Expressions

❧ 115 ❧

A cada gusto su susto.
    a. For every delight there is a fright.
    b. For every pleasant moment, there is an unpleasant
       moment.

❧ 116 ❧

Algo es algo.
    a. Something is something.
    b. Something is better than nothing.

❧ 117 ❧

Año de nones, año de dones.
    a. Odd years, gift years.
    b. Good things happen during odd years.

❧ 118 ❧

Asi es la vida.
    Such is life.

Cada cosa en su momento.
    a. Each thing in its moment.
    b. Everything has its time.

Cada cual en su nivel.
    a. Each one on his level.
    b. Each person to his station in life.
    c. Each person to his position in society.

Cada niño trae su torta.
    a. Each child brings his loaf.
    b. Each child brings his taco into this world.
    c. A way will be found to feed each child that is born.

Cada persona juzga por su condición.
    a. Each person judges by his own condition.
    b. Each person judges from his own perspective.

Con copa vacía no hay alegría.
    With an empty goblet, there is no joy.

Creer es poder.
    a. To believe is to have the power to do it.
    b. To believe is to achieve.

De este mundo llevarás panza llena y nada más.
    From this world you will take a full stomach and nothing else.

⁊ 126 ⁊

De tal jarro, tal tepalcate.
   a. From such a jug, such a jug fragment.
   b. From a given jug, a given jug fragment.
   c. The piece is similar to the whole.

⁊ 127 ⁊

De tal maguey, tal mezcal.
   a. From such a maguey (agave plant),
      such mescal (liquor).
   b. From a given plant, a given liquor.
   c. The product resembles the source.

⁊ 128 ⁊

El deber es el deber.
   a. A duty is a duty.
   b. A duty is a moral obligation.

⁊ 129 ⁊

El mundo es un pañuelo.
   a. The world is a handkerchief.
   b. There is sorrow in the
      world.

⁊ 130 ⁊

El que puede, puede.
   a. The one who can, can.
   b. Those who can, do.

⁊ 131 ⁊

El sol es la cobija de los pobres.
   a. The sun in the roof of the poor.
   b. The sun is the poor person's
      blanket.

El mundo es un pañuelo.

∽ 132 ∾

En gustos no hay disputa.
   a. In taste there is no dispute.
   b. Every person to his taste.
   c. There is no accounting for taste.

∽ 133 ∾

En la variedad está el gusto.
   a. In variety is found pleasure.
   b. Variety is the spice of life.

∽ 134 ∾

Es la gota que derramó el vaso.
   a. It's the drop of water that spilled from the glass.
   b. It's the straw that broke the camel's back.

∽ 135 ∾

La esperanza es la última que muere.
   Hope is the last to die.

∽ 136 ∾

La lucha se hace, la suerte es la mala.
   a. You can do the struggle; luck is the bad one.
   b. You can make the struggle, but you can't make luck.

∽ 137 ∾

La música domina las fieras.
   a. Music moderates the wild beasts.
   b. Music is soothing to all.

∽ 138 ∾

La necesidad es madre de invención.
   Necessity is the mother of invention.

❧ 139 ❦

La vida es corta—hay que vivirla.
Life is short—it is necessary to enjoy it.

❧ 140 ❦

La vida es para gozar.
Life is to be enjoyed.

❧ 141 ❦

Lo bueno dura poco.
a. The good lasts little.
b. The good lasts only a short time.
c. The good die young.

❧ 142 ❦

Lo que comienza mal, acaba mal.
That which begins badly, ends badly.

❧ 143 ❦

Lo que está puesto, nuestro.
a. What is put on is ours.
b. That which we wear is ours.
c. Possession is ownership.

❧ 144 ❦

Me dijo cuatro verdades.
a. He told me four truths.
b. He told me the way things are.

❧ 145 ❦

Mientras más se vive, más se ve.
a. The more you live, the more you see.
b. The longer you live, the more you experience.

146

No quiero ser juez de nadie.
    a. I don't want to be anyone's judge.
    b. I don't like to judge people.

147

No solo de pan vive el hombre.
    a. Not only from bread lives a man.
    b. Man does not live by bread alone.

148

No todo es vida y dulzura.
    a. Not everything is living and sweetness.
    b. Life has its ups and downs.

149

Para todo alcanza el tiempo sabiéndolo aprovechar.
    There is enough time for everything if one knows how to utilize one's time.

150

Por ese camino vamos todos.
    a. Along that road we all go.
    b. Down that road we all travel.
    c. In that direction all of us are heading.

151

Por mi raza habla el espíritu.
    a. Through my race speaks the spirit.
    b. Through my people speaks the soul.

≫ 152 ≪

Puede más el vicio que la razón.
   a. Vice can do more than reason.
   b. A bad habit can prevail over reason.

≫ 153 ≪

Recordar es vivir.
   a. To remember is to live.
   b. To remember is to relive.

≫ 154 ≪

Todo el rato que uno está enojado, pierde de estar contento.
   a. All the time that one is angry one loses a time to be content.
   b. When you are angry, you lose an opportunity to be joyful.

≫ 155 ≪

Todo se paga en este mundo.
   a. Everything is paid in this world.
   b. You are held accountable for everything that you do.

≫ 156 ≪

Una mano lava la otra y ambas la cara.
   a. One hand washes the other, and both wash the face.
   b. Today I help you, tomorrow you help me, and the day after, you and I help others.

Expresiones que aconsejan
Expressions That Advise

✋ 157 ✋

A cualquiera se le van las patas.
   a. Anyone can lose one's feet.
   b. Anyone can make a serious mistake.

✋ 158 ✋

A la mejor cocinera se le va un tomate entero.
   a. The best cook loses an entire tomato.
   b. We all make mistakes.

✋ 159 ✋

Al maguey que no da pulque, no hay que llevar acocate.
   a. Do not take a goard to the maguey (plant) that does not give pulque (liquor).
   b. Do not waste your time with things that do not produce.

✋ 160 ✋

A mal tiempo, buena cara.
   Keep a good face during bad times.

Al maguey que no da pulque, no hay que llevar acocate.

~ 161 ~

Amor, dinero, y cuidados, no pueden ser disimulados.
Love, money, and caring cannot be feigned.

~ 162 ~

Aquí las paredes oyen.
    a. Here the walls hear.
    b. Here the walls can hear.
    c. The walls have ears.

❧ 163 ❧

Cabestreas o te ahorcas.
   a. Follow the halter or you will hang.
   b. Follow the person who holds the rope or you will choke.
   c. Follow the leader or you will suffer.

❧ 164 ❧

Cada quien tiene su modo de apearse.
   a. Each one has his way of dismounting.
   b. Each person has his way of doing things.

❧ 165 ❧

Con la intención basta.
   a. With the intention is enough.
   b. The intention is sufficient.
   c. It's the thought that counts.

❧ 166 ❧

De bajada hasta las piedras ruedan.
   a. On the way down, even the stones roll.
   b. Going downhill has always been easy.

❧ 167 ❧

De golosos y tragones están llenos los panteones.
   Of gluttons and heavy drinkers, the cemeteries are full.

❧ 168 ❧

De los males, el menos.
   a. Of the evils, the least.
   b. If injury comes, let it be the least of injuries.

❧ 169 ❧

De vez en cuando, es necesario bailar con el diablo.
  a. From time to time, it is necessary to dance with the devil.
  b. Sometimes one must dance with danger.
  c. Sometimes we must do things that are against our principles.

❧ 170 ❧

El que es bilingüe vale por dos.
  The bilingual person is worth two.

❧ 171 ❧

El que no habla de flores no es jardinero.
  a. The one who does not talk about flowers is not a gardener.
  b. The person who does not discuss flowers is not a gardener.
  c. The person who does not discuss his work is not a master
     of his vocation.

❧ 172 ❧

El que quiera celeste, que le cueste.
  a. The one who wants light blue will have to pay.
  b. Good things are expensive.

❧ 173 ❧

El que viene muy seguido molesta.
  a. The person annoys who comes too often.
  b. The frequent visitor annoys the host.

❧ 174 ❧

Entre broma y broma la verdad se asoma.
  Between joke and jest, the truth appears.

❧ 175 ❧

Es peligroso jugar con fuego.
  It is dangerous to play with fire.

⚘ 176 ⚘

Hay que saber perder.
   a. One should know how to lose.
   b. One should know how to lose as well as win.

⚘ 177 ⚘

Júntate con los buenos y serás uno de ellos.
   a. Gather with the good ones and you will be one of them.
   b. Associate with good people and you too will be a good person.

⚘ 178 ⚘

Juzga a un hombre cuando te hayas puesto en su lugar.
   Judge a man when you have put yourself in his place.

⚘ 179 ⚘

Lo del agua, al agua.
   a. That which is from the water, returns to the water.
   b. Do not cry over a lost object that you had previously found, because it wasn't yours in the first place.
   c. It returned to its original place.

⚘ 180 ⚘

Lo pasado, pasado.
   a. The past passed.
   b. The past is forgiven and forgotten.
   c. That which has passed should be forgiven and forgotten.
   d. That's water under the bridge.

⚘ 181 ⚘

Lo que a uno cura, a otro mata.
   a. That which cures one person will kill another.
   b. One person's meat is another person's poison.

Los hombres no lloran, nomás pujan.
    Men do not cry, they just grunt. (This is said to a little boy to
    stop him from crying.)

Más vale callar que mucho hablar.
    It is better to be silent than to talk too much.

Ni limosnero ni ladrón.
    a. Neither a beggar nor a thief.
    b. Be neither a beggar nor a thief.

No andes con rodeos.
    a. Don't go about with evasions.
    b. Speak in a straightforward manner.

No andes por las ramas, vete directo al grano.
    a. Don't go to the branches, go directly to the seed.
    b. Don't beat around the bush, come to the point.

No con quien naces, sino con quien pases.
    a. Not with whom you are born, but with whom you spend
        time.
    b. You are known by the people with whom you associate.

No enseñes el cobre.
    a. Do not show the copper.
    b. Do not show your worse side.

No hay enemigo pequeño.
    a. There is no small enemy.
    b. There is no such thing as a minor enemy.

No hay un consejo que ande solo.
    a. There is no advice that comes alone.
    b. When you ask for advice, you will get more than you need.

No la hagas y no la dirán.
    Do not do it, and they will not say that you did it.

No le busques mangas al chaleco.
    a. Do not look for sleeves on the vest.
    b. Do not look for that which you will not find.

No le vayas hacer ojo.
    a. Do not cast the evil eye on him.
    b. Do not bring him bad luck.
    c. Do not jinx him.

No metas la cuchara.
    a. Do not put in your spoon.
    b. Stay out of it.
    c. Don't get involved in this matter.

❧ 195 ❧

No puedes tapar el sol con un dedo.
   a. You cannot cover the sun with one finger.
   b. Some problems require a large solution.

❧ 196 ❧

No quites el dedo del renglón.
   a. Don't take your finger from the line.
   b. Stay with it.

❧ 197 ❧

No revuelvan el agua.
   a. Do not stir up the water.
   b. Do not make waves.
   c. Do not cause problems.

❧ 198 ❧

No seas tan soflamero.
   a. Do not be such a sophist.
   b. Don't be so deceptive.
   c. Don't be so finicky.

❧ 199 ❧

No te metas en camisa de once varas.
   a. Do not get into a shirt of eleven yards.
   b. Don't get involved in a mess.

❧ 200 ❧

No te vayas a morder la lengua.
   a. Do not bite your tongue.
   b. Do not be critical of others if you share their faults.

¿Para qué andar con rodeos?
    a. Why go about with circumlocutions?
    b. Why don't we get right down to the heart of the matter?

Para que se acaben las chinches, hay que quemar el petate.
    To get rid of the bedbugs, one must burn the bed mat.

Piénsalo dos veces antes de dar el salto.
    Think twice before you leap.

Piensa mal y acertarás.
    a. Think of trouble and it will occur.
    b. Problems can occur from negative thinking.

¡Ponte muy aguila!
    a. Put yourself very eagle!
    b. Stay like an eagle!
    c. Stay alert!
    d. Be careful!

Predicas pero no aplicas.
    a. You preach, but you do not apply.
    b. You preach, but you do not practice what you preach.
    c. Practice what you preach.

✒ 207 ✒

Puerta que se abre, te llama.
   a. A door that opens calls you.
   b. A door that opens signifies an opportunity.

✒ 208 ✒

Secreto de dos, secreto de Dios; secreto de tres, de todos es.
   A secret between two is safe with God; a secret among three
      people is everyone's secret.

✒ 209 ✒

Se franco pero no tanto.
   a. Be frank, but not too much.
   b. Be frank, but not too frank.

✒ 210 ✒

Siempre espera lo peor.
   a. Always expect the worst.
   b. Always be ready for the worst thing that can happen.

✒ 211 ✒

Uno puede caminar en el lodo y salir limpio.
   a. One can walk in the mud and come out clean.
   b. A person can associate with the immoral and remain pure.

✒ 212 ✒

Vale más resbalar con los pies que con la lengua.
   a. It is better to slip with your feet than with your tongue.
   b. A slip of the foot is better than a slip of the tongue.

Expresiones religiosas
Religious Expressions

✎ 213 ✎

Bendito sea Dios.
   Blessed be God.

✎ 214 ✎

Como el beso de Judas.
   a. Like the kiss of Judas.
   b. He is as false as the kiss of Judas.

✎ 215 ✎

Con el favor de Dios.
   a. With God's favor.
   b. With the help of God.
   c. If God is willing.

✎ 216 ✎

Del agua mansa líbrame Dios, que de la brava me cuido yo.
   a. From the gentle water deliver me, God, because from the
      strong water I can protect myself.
   b. Protect me, God, from the small things, because the large
      things I can see.

ᗧ 217 ᗤ

Dios me libre.
God sets me free.

ᗧ 218 ᗤ

Dios no cumple antojos ni endereza jorobados. (humorístico)
God does not fulfill/grant whims nor straighten hunchbacks.
(humorous)

ᗧ 219 ᗤ

Dios por delante.
a. God in front.
b. May God lead the way.

ᗧ 220 ᗤ

El que no conoce a Dios, a cualquier santo se le hinca.
If one does not know God, one kneels before any saint.

ᗧ 221 ᗤ

Encomiéndate a Dios.
a. Entrust yourself to God.
b. Place yourself in God's hands.

ᗧ 222 ᗤ

¡Gracias a Dios!
a. Thank God!
b. Thank heaven!

ᗧ 223 ᗤ

La venganza es placer de dioses.
a. Vengeance is the pleasure of gods.
b. Vengeance is the function of God.

Lo hizo sin encomendarse a Dios ni al diablo.
  a. He did it without asking for the protection of God or the
     devil.
  b. He was foolhardy to get involved in that matter.

Que Dios la bendiga.
  May God bless you.

Que Dios lo tenga en su santa gloria.
  a. May God have him in His holy glory.
  b. May he be with God.

Que Dios te oiga.

Que Dios me agarre confesado.
   a. May God come upon me confessed.
   b. I hope that I am ready for God when my time comes.

Que Dios se lo page.
   May God repay you.

Que Dios te oiga.
   a. May God hear you.
   b. May God answer your prayers.

¿Quién dice que no hay Diosito?
   a. Who says there is no little God?
   b. Who says there is no God?
   c. Doesn't this prove that God exists?

Santo que no es visto no es adorado.
   The saint that is not seen is not adored.

Se dice el pecado, no el pecador.
   a. You tell the sin, not the sinner.
   b. You confess the sin but not the sinner's name.

Vive con el Jesus en la boca.
   a. He lives with Jesus in his mouth.
   b. He is always evoking the name of Jesus Christ.
   c. He lives in a state of uneasiness.

Expresiones acerca del amor
Expressions About Love

❧ 234 ❧

Amor con celos causa desvelos.
   a. Love with jealousy causes lack of sleep.
   b. The suspicious lover does not sleep well.

❧ 235 ❧

De mal de amor nadie se ha muerto.
   From the illness of love, no one has ever died.

❧ 236 ❧

El amor no cumple años.
   a. Love does not have a birthday.
   b. Sometimes love does not last a year.

❧ 237 ❧

El amor solo llega una vez.
   a. Love arrives only once.
   b. True loves comes only once.

Indio sin india, cuerpo sin alma.
    a. An Indian without a female Indian, a body without a soul.
    b. An Indian who doesn't have an Indian maiden to love is a
       body without a soul.

La que se muere, la entiero; y la que se va la olvido.
    a. The one who dies I will bury, and the one who leaves me I
       will forget.
    b. The woman who dies I will bury, and the woman who
       leaves me I will forget.

No hay amor sin interés.
    a. There is not love without interest.
    b. There is not love without concern for the future.
    c. Weigh all the factors before you make a commitment.

No se puede vivir nomás de amor.
    One cannot live just on love.

Para el mal de amores no hay doctores.
    a. For the illness of love there are no doctors.
    b. There is no remedy for the love bug.

Quien ama al feo, bonito le parece.
    a. Who loves the homely, pretty he appears.
    b. The homely person appears attractive to the one who loves
       him.

Expresiones acerca de las mujeres

Expressions About Women

❧ 244 ❧

El vino bueno y la mujer hermosa.
- a. Good wine and a beautiful woman.
- b. True pleasure consists of good wine and a beautiful woman.

❧ 245 ❧

Es chiquita pero picosa.
- a. She is small but she can sting.
- b. She is small but she is strong.
- c. She may be small but she can defend herself.

❧ 246 ❧

Es mucha carne para Juan. (humorístico)
- a. It's a lot of meat for John. (humorous)
- b. She's too much woman for him.

❧ 247 ❧

La mujer en sus quehaceres.
- a. A woman at her housework.
- b. A woman's place is in the home.

∽ 248 ∾

La mujer que nace bonita, nace casada.
The woman who is born pretty is born married.

∽ 249 ∾

Le dió calabazas.
   a. He gave her pumpkins.
   b. He jilted her.

∽ 250 ∾

Le echaron un piropo.
   a. They threw her a compliment.
   b. They paid her a compliment.

∽ 251 ∾

Le tiraron una flor.
   a. They threw her a flower.
   b. They paid her a compliment.

∽ 252 ∾

Lo que tiene de bonita, lo tiene de loca. (humorístico)
What she has in prettiness she has in craziness. (humorous)

∽ 253 ∾

Me gustan las bonitas por bonitas y las feas por feitas. (humorístico)
   a. I like the pretty ones because they are pretty, and the
      homely ones because they are homely. (humorous)
   b. I like pretty girls because they are pretty, and I like the
      homely girls because they are homely. (humorous)

∽ 254 ∾

Me gustan las gorditas y las flaquitas también. (humorístico)
   a. I like thick tortillas and the thin ones, too.
   b. I like plump girls and the skinny ones, too. (humorous)

∽ 255 ∾

Mujeres juntas, solo difuntas. (humorístico)
    a. Women together, only deceased. (humorous)
    b. Women should be together only when they are deceased.
       (humorous)

∽ 256 ∾

No hay bonita sin pero, ni fea sin gracia. (humorístico)
    a. There is not a pretty woman without a "but" nor a homely
       one without beauty.
    b. There is not a pretty woman without a defect nor a homely
       one without good qualities.

∽ 257 ∾

No hay fea que no tenga gracia, ni bonito sin defecto.
    There is not a homely woman who does not have grace nor a
    pretty woman without a defect.

Expresiones acerca del matrimonio
Expressions About Marriage

❧ 258 ❧

El casado casa quiere.
The married person wants a house.

❧ 259 ❧

El que no la corre de soltero la corre de casado. (humorístico)
The person who does not run (carouse) as a bachelor runs (carouses) as a married man. (humorous)

❧ 260 ❧

Estoy casado por las tres leyes—por la iglesia, por el civil, y por tonto. (humorístico)
I am married by the three laws—by the church, by civil law, and by stupidity. (humorous)

❧ 261 ❧

Más vale mal casada que bien quedada. (humorístico)
It is better to marry poorly/badly than to be left unmarried. (humorous)

Expresiones tocante al hogar
Expressions About the Home

⁓ 262 ⁓

A la mesa y a la cama, nomás una vez se llama.
To the table and to bed only once is one called.

⁓ 263 ⁓

Bienvenidos a nuestro hogar.
Welcome to our home.

⁓ 264 ⁓

¿Cedacito nuevo, dónde te pondré?
   a. New little sieve, where shall I place you?
   b. Now, where should I place my new possession?

⁓ 265 ⁓

De la puerta al rincón todo es colchón. (humorístico)
   a. From the door to the corner, everything is mattress.
   b. Their home is full of beds.
   c. There is always room for another overnight guest in their
      home.

El que no repara la gotera, repara la casa entera.
    a. The one who does not repair the leak repairs the entire house.
    b. A stitch in time saves nine.

Esta es su casa.
    a. This is your home.
    b. You are welcome in our home.
    c. Welcome to our home.
    d. Consider our home your home.

Pásenle a lo barrido.

✎ 268 ✎

Pásenle a lo barrido. (humorístico)
a. Pass into an area that has been swept.
b. Please come into a recently swept house. (humorous)

✎ 269 ✎

Quien viene a mesa puesta no sabe lo que cuesta.
a. The person who comes to a set table does not know what it costs.
b. Much effort and expense is involved in preparing a meal for someone.

✎ 270 ✎

Se me pegaron las cobijas.
a. The bed blankets stuck to me.
b. I couldn't get out of bed.

Expresiones acerca de la familia

Expressions About the Family

✢ 271 ✢

Allí nomás donde vea la suegra. (humorístico)
  a. Only there where the mother-in-law will see.
  b. I will clean the house only in those places where my mother-in-law (and other guests) will notice. (humorous)

✢ 272 ✢

Bendita sea la que haya tenido tan buen hijo.
  Blessed be the one (woman) who gave birth to such a good son.

✢ 273 ✢

Es el coyotito.
  a. He is the little coyote.
  b. He is the youngest child in the family.

✢ 274 ✢

Que viva mi suegra, pero que viva bien lejos. (humorístico)
  Long live my mother-in-law, but may she live far away. (humorous)

Expresiones acerca del trabajo
Expressions About Work

❧ 275 ❧

Ahora sí, a echarme las naguas a la cabeza.
- a. Now to throw my skirt to my head.
- b. It's time to get to work.

❧ 276 ❧

A *rey muerto, rey puesto.*
- a. A dead king, a king placed.
- b. One king dies and another king succeeds.
- c. When one boss leaves, another boss arrives.

❧ 277 ❧

A *todo le tira y a nada le pega.*
- a. He throws at everything and hits nothing.
- b. He tries everything but succeeds at nothing.
- c. He is a jack of all trades and a master of none.

A trabajar se ha dicho.
   a. To work, it has been said.
   b. It's time to return to work.

Busca trabajo rogando a Dios no hallarlo. (humorístico)
   He seeks work, praying to God that he will not find it. (humorous)

Es el chambón de los chambones.
   a. He is the clumsy of the clumsy workers.
   b. He is the most unskilled of all the unskilled workers.
   c. He is an awkward worker.

Lo hizo como sus patas.
   a. He did it like his feet.
   b. He did the work as if he had done it with his feet.
   c. He did a terrible job.

Expresiones tocante a los oficios
Expressions About Occupations

⁓ 282 ⁓

Es mesero sin charola. (humorístico)
   a. He is a waiter without a tray. (humorous)
   b. He has the appearance of a waiter.

⁓ 283 ⁓

Témele más a los abogados que a los pleitos.
   a. Fear more the lawyers than the disputes.
   b. Fear more the lawyer than the lawsuit.

⁓ 284 ⁓

Zapatero a tus zapatos.
   a. Shoemaker to your shoes.
   b. A shoemaker should concentrate on making shoes.
   c. Each person should mind his own business.

Expresiones acerca de los negocios

Expressions About Business

~ 285 ~

Con su palabra basta.
   a. With your word is enough.
   b. Your word suffices.
   c. Your promise is sufficient.

~ 286 ~

Entre dos amigos un notario y dos testigos.
   a. Among two friends, a notary public and two witnesses.
   b. When two friends enter into an agreement, utilize a notary
      public and two witnessess.

~ 287 ~

Le pagaron en tres plazos: tarde, mal, y nunca. (humorístico)
   They paid him in three installments: late, poorly (partially),
      and never. (humorous)

Lo hizo para taparle el ojo al macho.
    a. He did it to cover the eye of the male.
    b. He did the job just well enough to have it accepted.

Me lo dió de pilón.
    a. He gave it to me extra.
    b. He gave it to me in appreciation for my purchase.
    c. He gave me something free as a sign of appreciation for my business.

Negocio que no deja, déjalo.
    a. Business that doesn't leave, leave it.
    b. Leave a business that doesn't leave a profit.

No me vendas vaca que tenga plumas. (humorístico)
    a. Do not sell me a cow that has feathers. (humorous)
    b. Do not deceive me on this transaction.
    c. Be honest with me.

Salir a mano es ganancia.
    a. To come out even is to profit.
    b. The person who breaks even gains.
    c. The person who breaks even in a business venture profits from the venture.

Expresiones tocante al dinero
Expressions About Money

⚘ 293 ⚘

Con el dinero no se olvidan los encargos.
   a. With money, errands are not neglected.
   b. When money is the stimulus, orders are not forgotten.

⚘ 294 ⚘

Dime cuanto traes y te diré cuanto vales. (humorístico)
   a. Tell me how much you have and I will tell you how much you are worth. (humorous)
   b. Tell me how much money you have in your pockets and I will tell you how much you are worth. (humorous)

⚘ 295 ⚘

Echaron la casa por la ventana.
   a. They threw the house through the window.
   b. They spent a great deal of money on the occasion.

⚘ 296 ⚘

El dinero atrae dinero.
   Money attracts money.

El *dinero mueve montañas.*
Money moves mountains.

El *oro siempre llama el oro.*
a. Gold always attracts gold.
b. Money attracts money.

El *que ha de ser centavo, aunque ande entre los billetes. (humorístico)*
The one who was meant to be a penny will not benefit from
associating with bills. (humorous)

El *que presta dinero a un amigo pierde el dinero y el amigo.*
The one who lends money to a friend loses the money and
the friend.

Es *más difícil guardarlo que ganarlo.*
a. It is more difficult to save it than to earn it.
b. It is more difficult to save money than to earn money.

Está *podrido en dinero.*
a. He's rotting in money.
b. He's filthy rich.

Estoy *bruja.*
I am broke.

❧ 304 ❧

Me salió con que el colchón no tiene lana.
   a. He told me that the mattress does not contain wool.
   b. He claims that he had no money in his bank account.

❧ 305 ❧

Mucho trabajo, poco dinero.
   a. Much work, little money.
   b. Much work, little pay.

❧ 306 ❧

¡Ni por todo el dinero en el mundo!
   a. Not for all the money in the world!
   b. I would not do it for all the money in the world.

❧ 307 ❧

No hay más amigo que Dios, ni más pariente que el dinero.
(humorístico)
   There is not a better friend than God nor a better relative
      than money. (humorous)

❧ 308 ❧

No le suena un centavo en la bolsa.
   a. A cent doesn't ring in his pocket.
   b. He doesn't have a penny to his name.

❧ 309 ❧

Para eso se hizo el dinero de papel—para volar. (humorístico)
   a. That is why money was made of paper—to fly. (humorous)
   b. Money was made of paper so that it could fly/circulate
      from person to person.

❧ 310 ❧

Para eso se hizo el dinero redondo—para rodar. (humorístico)
 a. That is why money was made round—to roll. (humorous)
 b. Coins were made round so that they could roll/circulate/be spent.

❧ 311 ❧

Por un centavo no se completa un peso.
 a. For one cent, you do not complete a peso.
 b. For the lack of one penny you do not complete a dollar.

❧ 312 ❧

Que bonito es lo limpio, menos en la bolsa. (humorístico)
 a. How beautiful is clean except in one's purse. (humorous)
 b. It is beautiful to be clean except when one's purse is clean (empty). (humorous)

❧ 313 ❧

Tiene dinero para aventar para arriba.
 a. He has money to throw into the air.
 b. He has plenty of money.
 c. He has money to burn.

❧ 314 ❧

Tiene más lana que un borrego.
 a. He has more wool than a lamb.
 b. He is loaded with money.

❧ 315 ❧

Tiene mucha lana.
 a. He/she has much wool.
 b. He/she has much money.

Expresiones acerca de los alimentos
Expressions About Food

≈ 316 ≈

Aquí nomás mis enchiladas tienen queso. (humorístico)
   a. Here only my enchiladas contain cheese.
   b. At this place only my enchiladas are filled with cheese.
   c. Only I have influence here.

≈ 317 ≈

Arroz que no se menea, se quema. (consejo)
   a. Rice that is not stirred will burn. (advice)
   b. One should not neglect his affairs.

≈ 318 ≈

Comes frijoles y repites pollo. (humorístico)
   a. You eat beans and belch chicken.
   b. You eat beans and dream of chicken.
   c. You eat beans and claim you ate chicken. (humorous)

Como agua pa' chocolate.

∽ 319 ∽

Como agua pa' chocolate.
  a. Like water for chocolate.
  b. He's like water for chocolate.
  c. He is hot under the collar.

∽ 320 ∽

Cuando hay hambre, no hay mal pan.
  When there is hunger, there is no bad bread.

∽ 321 ∽

Donde come uno, comen dos.
  a. From which one can eat, two can eat.
  b. Two can eat as cheaply as one.

✍ 322 ✍

Donde come uno, comen dos pero comen menos. (humorístico)
    a. From which one can eat, two can eat, but they eat less.
       (humorous)
    b. Two can eat as cheaply as one, but they will eat less. (humorous)

✍ 323 ✍

Échenle más agua al caldo. (humorístico)
    a. Put more water in the soup.
    b. Add water to the soup, because more guests are coming.
       (humorous)

✍ 324 ✍

El que no quiera caldo, taza y media. (humorístico)
    a. For the person who doe not want soup, a cup and a half.
    b. Reserve a cup and a half of soup for the person who says
       he does not want soup. (humorous)

✍ 325 ✍

Es arroz comido.
    a. It is rice eaten.
    b. It's as good as done.
    c. It's a feat accomplished.

✍ 326 ✍

Es como el ajonjolí—en todos los moles anda.
    a. He is like sesame—he is found in all the moles. (Mole is a
       Mexican dish of turkey/chicken with gravy.)
    b. He can be found everywhere.

✍ 327 ✍

Ese arroz ya se coció.
    a. That rice is cooked.
    b. The time is right.

ᕱ 328 ᕱ

Es más viejo que el caldo. (humorístico)
   a. He is older than the broth. (humorous)
   b. He is older than the soup on the stove. (humorous)

ᕱ 329 ᕱ

Es pan comido.
   a. That is bread that has been eaten.
   b. This is going to be a pleasure.

ᕱ 330 ᕱ

Está hasta en la sopa.
   a. He's even in the soup.
   b. He's into everything.
   c. He's a bothersome person.

ᕱ 331 ᕱ

Es tan pobre como el atole blanco.
   He is as poor as white atole (a drink made of corn meal).

ᕱ 332 ᕱ

No hay caldo que no se enfríe.
   a. There is not a soup that will not cool.
   b. Things can change.

ᕱ 333 ᕱ

No sabe ni con cuantas gordas llena.
   a. He does not know how many thick corn tortillas will fill him.
   b. He does not know his own limits.
   c. He lacks self-understanding.

Pa' frijoles en mi casa. (humorístico)
   a. For beans in my house.
   b. I can eat beans at home.
   c. Beans I can eat at home. Let's eat something else.

Para esa tos, frijoles con arroz. (humorístico)
   a. For that cough, beans with rice. (humorous)
   b. To cure that cough, eat beans with rice. (humorous)

Peor es chile y agua lejos. (humorístico)
   a. Worse is chile and water far away.
   b. A worse situation is eating chile with water far away.
      (humorous)
   c. Things could be worse.

Puso toda la carne en el asador.
   a. He put all the meat in the oven.
   b. He exerted his best effort.

Se comió la torta antes de hacerla.
   a. He ate the cake before making it.
   b. He spent the money before he earned it.

Tras de la sopa, la copa.
   a. After the soup, the drinking glass.
   b. After the soup, a glass of wine.

Expresiones acerca
de las relaciones humanas
Expressions About Human Relations

∾ 340 ∾

Ahora me cumples o me dejas como estaba.
    a. Now you fulfill or you leave me as I was.
    b. Marry me now or leave me.

∾ 341 ∾

Comen del mismo plato.
    a. They eat from the same plate.
    b. They are very close.
    c. Those two are great friends.

∾ 342 ∾

Hacen buenas migas.
    a. They make good bread crumbs.
    b. They get along.

∾ 343 ∾

Juntos pero no revueltos.
    a. Together but not mixed up.
    b. We may socialize, but we do not sleep in the same bed.

Comen del mismo plato.

~ 344 ~

La paso pero no la trago.
   a. I swallow her but I do not like her.
   b. I can tolerate her but I dislike her.

~ 345 ~

Me dió la patada.
   a. He gave me the kick.
   b. He left me.
   c. He dropped me.

✑ 346 ✑

No me pueden ver ni en pintura.
  a. They can't even see me in a painting.
  b. They can't stand the sight of me.

✑ 347 ✑

Se tapan con la misma colcha.
  a. They cover themselves with the same blanket.
  b. They are very close.

✑ 348 ✑

Son como uña y carne.
  a. They are like fingernail and flesh.
  b. They are very close.

Expresiones descriptivas
Descriptive Expressions

❧ 349 ❧

Acaba de salir del cascarón.
   a. He has just come out of the eggshell.
   b. He's young and inexperienced.

❧ 350 ❧

Amaneció con el pico caído.
   a. He awakened with a fallen beak.
   b. He woke up in a bad mood.

❧ 351 ❧

Anda armado hasta por los dientes.
   He/she is armed to the teeth.

❧ 352 ❧

Anda de boca en boca.
   a. He is going about from mouth to mouth.
   b. They are talking about him.

Anda de pata de perro.
  a. He is going about like a dog's foot.
  b. He is out on the town.

Anda más alborotado que una gallina clueca.
  He is more excited than a brooding hen.

A planchar oreja.
  a. To smooth out the ear.
  b. Let us smooth out the ear.
  c. It is time to sleep.

A ver quien lleva los pantalones.
  a. Let's see who wears the pants.
  b. Let's see who is in charge here.

Desnuda un santo para vestir otro.
  a. He undresses one saint to dress another.
  b. He takes from one to give to another.
  c. He robs Peter to pay Paul.

De tal filo es mi machete.
  a. Such a cutting edge has my machete.
  b. My machete is always ready.

ॐ 359 ॐ

El asunto no tiene pies ni cabeza.
    a. The matter does not have feet nor a head.
    b. The matter does not make sense.

ॐ 360 ॐ

Es como buscar una aguja en un pajar.
    a. It is like looking for a needle in a straw loft.
    b. It is like looking for a needle in a haystack.

ॐ 361 ॐ

Es feo con efe mayúcula. (humorístico)
    He is ugly with a capital U. (humorous)

ॐ 362 ॐ

Es feo, fuerte, y formal.
    He is unattractive, strong, and formal. (humorous)

ॐ 363 ॐ

Está con un pie en la sepultura.
    a. He has one foot in the grave.
    b. He is in bad health.

ॐ 364 ॐ

Está en los brazos de Morfeo.
    a. He is in the arms of Morpheus.
    b. He is asleep.
    c. He is sound asleep.

ॐ 365 ॐ

Están cortados con las mismas tijeras.
    a. They are cut with the same scissors.
    b. They are very much alike.
    c. They are two of a kind.

❧ 366 ❧

Está vivita y coleando.
    a. She is alive and wagging her tail.
    b. She is alive and kicking.
    c. She is doing well.

❧ 367 ❧

Es un angelito con cuernos.
    He is a little angel with horns.

❧ 368 ❧

Es un pan bendito.
    a. He is a holy bread.
    b. He is a saint.
    c. He is extremely virtuous.

❧ 369 ❧

Habla con el corazón en la mano.
    a. He speaks with his heart in his hand.
    b. He speaks from the heart.

❧ 370 ❧

Habla hasta por los codos.
    a. He speaks even from his elbows.
    b. He is very talkative.

❧ 371 ❧

La pescaron con las manos en la masa.
    a. They caught her with her hands in the dough.
    b. They caught her in the act.
    c. They caught her with her hand in the cookie jar.

La pescaron con las manos en la masa.

372

Le echó leña al fuego.
  a. He threw firewood to the fire.
  b. He added fuel to the flame.

373

Le picó los ojos.
  a. She pierced his eyes.
  b. She made a fool of him.

374

Le sacaron las garritas asolear.
  a. They took out her little cloths to dry in the sun.
  b. Her cloth remnants were put in the sunlight.
  c. Her transgressions were made public.

375

Le sumieron un ojo.
  a. They shriveled one of his eyes.
  b. They took advantage of him.
  c. They overcharged him.

376

Los mirones son de palo.
  a. Onlookers are made of wood.
  b. Onlookers do not contribute.

377

Me quedé con la pata lavada.
  a. I was left with my foot washed.
  b. I washed my feet and then had no place to go.
  c. I took a bath and then I was stood up.
  d. I got ready and then had no place to go.

Me saludó de los dientes pa' fuera.
   a. He greeted me from the teeth outward.
   b. He greeted me reluctantly.
   c. He gave me a cold greeting.

Mete la cuchara en todo.
   a. He puts his spoon into everything.
   b. He sticks his spoon/nose into everybody's business.

Metí la pata.
   a. I put in the foot,
   b. I put my foot in it.
   c. I said something I shouldn't have.

No aflojó un pelo.
   a. He did not let go of a hair.
   b. He did not let go of a single hair.
   c. He did not give an inch.

No me busques canas verdes, que no tengo ni una.
   a. Don't look for green grey hair on me, for I have not a one.
   b. Please don't take me for a fool.

No se mama el dedo.
   a. He does not suck his finger.
   b. He does not suck his thumb.
   c. He is not easily fooled.

❧ 384 ❧

No tiene pelos en la lengua.
   a. He doesn't have hair on his tongue.
   b. He tells it like it is.

❧ 385 ❧

Parece gallina remojada.
   She looks like a soaked chicken.

❧ 386 ❧

Parece león enjaulado.
   a. He seems like a caged lion.
   b. He acts like a caged lion.

❧ 387 ❧

Parece mosca en leche. (humorístico)
   a. She looks like a fly in milk. (humorous)
   b. She looks like a fly in a glass of milk. (humorous)

❧ 388 ❧

Parece que le sacan las palabras con tirabuzón.
   a. It seems that they pull out the words with a corkscrew.
   b. It is difficult to get him to say anything.
   c. He is tightlipped.

❧ 389 ❧

Pidió la mano y tomó el pie.
   a. He asked for the hand and he took a foot.
   b. He asked for a hand and he took a foot.
   c. He took more than he requested.

¿Quién te mete, Juan Copete?
    a. Who gets you in, Juan Copete?
    b. Who got you into this conversation, Juan Copete?
    c. Who invited you into this conversation, John Pompadour?

Se chupó los dedos.
    a. He sucked his fingers.
    b. He ate with much pleasure.

Se hizo ojo de hormiga.
    a. He made himself an ant's eye.
    b. He made himself scarce.

Se hizo tortilla.
    a. He became a tortilla.
    b. He sat down and wouldn't get up.
    c. (It also means "He fell down flat as a pancake.")

Se le metió por el ojo.
    a. It got in him through the eye.
    b. He became fixated on a person (or thing).

Se le salen las cosas como a las guitarras viejas.
    a. Things come out of him as they do from old guitars.
    b. Words come out of him like sounds come out of an old
       guitar.

396

Se levantó con el sombrero atravesado.
   a. He awoke with the hat crossed.
   b. He awake in a bad mood.

397

Se me puso la piel como carne de gallina.
   a. My skin became like hen flesh.
   b. I developed goosebumps.

398

Tiene cara de gamuza. (humorístico)
   a. He has a face like a chamois.
   b. He has a face like a dry chamois. (humorous)
   c. His face is extremely wrinkled.

399

Tiene nariz de chile verde. (humorístico)
   a. He has a nose like a green pepper. (humorous)
   b. His nose resembles a green pepper. (humorous)

400

Tiene ojos de chivo empachado. (humorístico)
   a. He has the eyes of a stuffed goat. (humorous)
   b. His eyes resemble those of a stuffed goat. (humorous)

401

Tiene orejas de papalote. (humorístico)
   a. He has ears like a kite. (humorous)
   b. He has protrusive ears.

402

Tiene panza de músico. (humorístico)
   He has the belly of a musician. (humorous)

✒ 403 ✒

Tiene pie de abanico. (humorístico)
    a. He has a foot like a hand fan. (humorous)
    b. He has wide feet.

✒ 404 ✒

Trató de lavarme la cara.
    a. He tried to wash my face.
    b. He tried to coax me with flattery.

✒ 405 ✒

Vió al diablo por un agujero.
    a. He saw the devil through a hole.
    b. He saw the devil close at hand.
    c. He found himself very close to danger.

Expresiones acerca de la condición humana
Expressions About the Human Condition

❧ 406 ❧

Al enfermo lo que pida.
   a. To the patient, whatever he asks.
   b. Give the ill person whatever he wants.

❧ 407 ❧

Al flojo Dios lo ayuda.
   a. God helps the lazy.
   b. It appears that God often helps the lazy.

❧ 408 ❧

Anda con una mano atrás y otra adelante.
   a. He is going about with one hand behind and another forward.
   b. He doesn't have a nickel in his pocket.

❧ 409 ❧

Ando de mal en peor.
   I am going from bad to worse.

Cada quien se arropa hasta donde le alcanza la cobija.
  a. Each person covers himself as far as the blanket reaches.
  b. Each person lives as far as his means will allow.

Da el largo pero no el ancho.
  a. He gives the length but not the width.
  b. He has the height but not the depth.
  c. He may be handsome but he lacks character.

Da mucha guerra.
  a. He gives much war.
  b. He bothers people.
  c. He causes much trouble.

De la uva que fué, solo queda una pasa.
  a. Of the grape that was, only a raisin remains.
  b. He is only a shadow of his former self.

De músico, poeta, y loco, todos tenemos un poco. (humorístico)
  a. Of the musician, poet, and lunatic, we all have a little.
  b. We all have in us a little of the musician, poet, and
    lunatic. (humorous)

De tan buenas no sirven.
  They are so good that they are useless.

El que solo se rie, de sus maldades se acuerda.
The person who laughs alone is remembering his past
  mischief.

Entre más viejos, más ridículos.
  a. The older, the more ridiculous.
  b. As we grow older, we become more strange.
  c. We become more laughable as we get older.

Es la sal de la vida.
  a. He is the salt of life.
  b. He is the salt of the earth.

Es más listo que un coyote.
He/she is more clever than a coyote.

Es más pobre que el pozole.
  a. He is poorer than pozole. (Pozole is a Mexican stew made
    of corn and pork.)
  b. He is as poor as grits.
  c. He is as poor as a church mouse.

Es muy codo.
  a. He is very elbow.
  b. He is very stingy.
  c. He is tight with his money.

Es muy hablador.
    a. He is very talkative.
    b. He is a big gossiper.

Está del mediodía pa' 'bajo.
    a. He is midday down.
    b. He is over the hill.

Está en las nubes.
    a. He is in the clouds.
    b. He's in another world.

Está más pa' allá que pa' acá.
    a. He is more over there than over here.
    b. He's over the hill.

Estoy entre la espada y la pared.
    a. I am between the sword and the wall.
    b. I am between a rock and a hard place.
    c. I am in a difficult position.

Es una chispa.
    a. He is a spark.
    b. He is all spirit.
    c. He is full of life.

⤟ 428 ⤞

Es un bendito.
    a. He is a saint.
    b. He is a good person.

⤟ 429 ⤞

Es un cero a la izquierda. (humorístico)
    a. He is a zero to the left. (humorous)
    b. He's a nobody.

⤟ 430 ⤞

Es un estuche de monerías.
    She is a jewel box of graciousness.

⤟ 431 ⤞

Es un hombre hecho y derecho.
    a. He is a man, made and straight.
    b. He is mature and just.

⤟ 432 ⤞

Es un pica buche.
    a. He is a craw pecker.
    b. He likes to stir up trouble.

⤟ 433 ⤞

Es un saca vueltas.
    a. He is a "take turns."
    b. He makes many turns before he gets the job done.
    c. He is a procrastinator.

❧ 434 ❧

Es un "tragaños."
   a. He's a "year-swallower."
   b. He swallows the years.
   c. He does not show his age.

❧ 435 ❧

Habla por hablar.
   a. He/she talks for the sake of talking.
   b. He/she talks to hear himself/herself talk.

❧ 436 ❧

Hasta de su sombra se asusta.
   a. Even of his shadow he is frightened.
   b. He is scared of his shadow.
   c. He is afraid of his own shadow.

❧ 437 ❧

La canasta está muy bajita.
   a. The basket is very low.
   b. The basket of food is very low.
   c. He doesn't make an effort to support himself, because his
      basic needs are being met.

❧ 438 ❧

Lanza la piedra y esconde la mano.
He throws the stone and hides the hand.

❧ 439 ❧

Las palabras me entran por un oído y me salen por el otro.
   a. The words go in one ear and out the other.
   b. I am not going to listen to what they say.

440

Le van alzar la canasta.
- a. They are going to raise his basket.
- b. They will elevate his basket of bread/food.
- c. They are going to make it more difficult for him to eat from the family food supply.
- d. They want him to start supporting himself.

441

Lo haré por la buena o por la mala.
- a. I will do it by the good or by the bad.
- b. I will do it by hook or crook.

442

Lo traen como badajo.
- a. They're treating him like a bell clapper.
- b. They've got him going left and right.

443

Me duele la cabeza, me duele el corazón. Me duele todo el cuerpo y los callos de pilón. (poético y humorístico)
- a. My head hurts, my heart hurts. All my body hurts, and so do my corns. (humorous)
- b. I am very tired.

444

¡Me lleva el diablo!
- a. The devil is taking me!
- b. I'm very angry.

445

¡Me lleva el tren!
- a. The train is taking me!
- b. I'm in desperate straits!

446

Me tomaron el pelo.
   a. They took my hair.
   b. They fooled me.

447

Me trae por la calle de la amargura.
   a. She is leading me down the street of bitterness.
   b. She is bringing grief to my life.

448

Nació con buena estrella.
   a. He was born with a good star.
   b. He was born lucky.

449

Nació con cuchara de oro en la boca.
   He was born with a gold spoon in his mouth.

450

No es cojo ni manco.
   a. He is neither a cripple nor one-armed.
   b. He is able to perform the task.

451

No hay ladrón que no sea desconfiado.
   There is not a thief who is not suspicious.

452

No hay ladrón que no sea llorón.
   a. There is not a thief that is not a crybaby.
   b. Thieves whine when they are caught.
   c. Thieves make excuses for their condition.

453

No puede negar la cruz de su parroquia.
   a. He can not deny the cross of his parish.
   b. He cannot deny his culture.

454

No quiero estar en tu pellejo.
   a. I do not want to be in your skin.
   b. I would not want to be in your position.
   c. I am glad I am not in your shoes.

455

No se aguanta ni solo.
   a. He can not endure himself.
   b. He can not stand himself.
   c. He can not even get along with himself.

456

No tiene cara con que hablar.
   a. He doesn't have a face with which to speak.
   b. He is in no position to criticize anyone.

457

No tiene donde caerse muerto.
   a. He does not have a place to fall dead.
   b. He is broke.

458

No tiene la culpa el pulque sino el ebrio que la bebe.
   a. The pulque (liquor) is not to blame but the drunk who
      drinks it.
   b. The drinker is to blame, not the liquor.

≈ 459 ≈

No tiene más que el pellejo.
   a. He has only his skin.
   b. He is penniless.
   c. He is destitute.

≈ 460 ≈

No tiene ni cara en que persignarse.
   a. He doesn't have enough face on which to make the sign of the cross.
   b. He lacks integrity.

≈ 461 ≈

No vale un pito.
   a. He is not worth a whistle.
   b. He is not worth a cent.
   c. He's worthless.

≈ 462 ≈

Otra vez la misma danza, y yo que no sé bailar.
   a. Again the same dance, and I who do not know how to dance.
   b. I missed another opportunity.

≈ 463 ≈

Pagó con su pellejo.
   a. He paid with his skin.
   b. He paid with his life.

≈ 464 ≈

Palabras de borracho, oídos de cantinero.
   a. Words of a drunkard, ears of a bartender.
   b. The words of a drunkard are heard by the bartender.

❧ 465 ❧

Para tonto no se estudia.
    a. To be a fool, you need not study.
    b. To be a fool, no preparation is required.

❧ 466 ❧

Parece alma que lleva el diablo.
    a. He seems like a soul taken by the devil.
    b. He seems to be under the devil's influence.
    c. He appears to be in a big hurry.

❧ 467 ❧

Parece mosquita muerta.
    a. She looks like a dead fly.
    b. She appears to be timid.

❧ 468 ❧

Parece tronco de amarrar burros. (humorístico)
    a. He resembles a tree trunk where you tie burros. (humorous)
    b. He is extremely short.

❧ 469 ❧

Pedro la hace y Juan la paga.
    a. Peter does it and John pays for it.
    b. One person commits the act and another is punished.
    c. One person commits the act and the rest pay.

❧ 470 ❧

Por eso estamos como estamos.
    a. That is why we are the way we are.
    b. That is the reason that we find ourselves in our present condition.

✽ 471 ✽

Pueblo chico, infierno grande.
Small town, large hell.

✽ 472 ✽

Que pronto se impone uno a lo bueno.
a. How quickly one becomes accustomed to the good.
b. How quickly one gets used to the good things in life.

✽ 473 ✽

Que pronto se le bajaron los humos.
a. How quickly did his pride go down.
b. His vanity fell quickly.

✽ 474 ✽

Regresó con el rabo entre las piernas.
He returned with his tail between his legs.

✽ 475 ✽

Salió con su domingo siete.
a. He came out with a Sunday seven.
b. He said something completely illogical.
c. He made an unreasonable statement.

✽ 476 ✽

Se cree la divina garza. (humorístico)
a. She thinks she is the divine heron. (humorous)
b. She has a high opinion of herself.

✽ 477 ✽

Se echó para atrás.
a. He threw backward.
b. He went back on his word.

93

Se cree la divina garza.

❦ 478 ❦

Se están ahorcando solos.
a. They are hanging themselves.
b. They are talking themselves into trouble.
c. Give them enough rope and they will hang themselves.

❦ 479 ❦

Se le fueron las patas.
a. Her feet went.
b. She made an impulsive decision.

Se le metió el diablo.
   a. The devil got into him.
   b. He started misbehaving.

Se le pasó el tren.
   a. The train passed him by.
   b. He missed the train.
   c. He missed an opportunity.

Se puso cara de vaqueta.
   a. He put on a face of leather.
   b. He hid his true feelings.
   c. He put up a front.

Se quedó para vestir santos. (humorístico)
   a. She stayed to dress saints.
   b. She never married.
   c. She remained an old maid.

Se roba a si mismo.
   a. He steals from himself.
   b. He'll steal from anyone.

Soy pobre pero honrado.
   I am poor but honest.

❧ 486 ❧

¡Tantos indios sin guaraches!
    a. So many Indians without sandals!
    b. There are a lot of poor people in this town.

❧ 487 ❧

Tiene cara de chicharrón.
    a. He has a face like a crackling.
    b. He has a rough complexion.

❧ 488 ❧

Tiene la música por dentro.
    a. He has music on the inside.
    b. He is a happy person, but he doesn't show it.

❧ 489 ❧

Tiene mucha cola que le pisen.
    a. He has much tail that they can step on.
    b. There is much about him that can be criticized.

❧ 490 ❧

Tiene mucho pico.
    a. He has much beak.
    b. He is very talkative.

❧ 491 ❧

Unos como saben y otros como pueden.
    a. Some since they know and others since they can.
    b. Some do because they know how to do it and others do
       because they can.
    c. Some can do it because they studied and others simply can
       do it.

∽ 492 ∾

Ya ni llorar es bueno.
   a. Now not even crying is useful.
   b. It is too late to cry.

∽ 493 ∾

¿Y crees tú que yo estoy en un lecho de rosas?
   a. And you believe that I am in a bed of roses?
   b. Why do you believe that my life is a bed of roses?

Expresiones casuales
Casual Expressions

∼ 494 ∼

¡A lo macho!
   a. Like a man!
   b. For real!
   c. I give you my word as a man.
   d. I give you my word.

∼ 495 ∼

A otro tonto con ese cuento.
   a. To another fool with that tale.
   b. Tell that story to someone else.
   c. I don't believe that story.

∼ 496 ∼

Aquí viene el mero mero.
   a. Here comes the real real.
   b. Here comes number one.
   c. Here comes the big boss.

497

A ver si como duermen, roncan.
    a. Let's see if how they sleep they snore.
    b. Let's see if they sleep the way they snore.
    c. Let's see if what they say is true.

498

Barájenmela más despacio.
    a. Shuffle more slowly for me.
    b. Shuffle the cards more slowly.
    c. Please elucidate.

499

Caeron como lluvia del cielo.
    a. They fell like rain from heaven.
    b. They came in bunches.

500

Cero y va una.
    a. Zero and there goes one.
    b. Here we go again.

501

¿De dónde cojieron agua las nubes?
    a. From where did the clouds get rain?
    b. Where did this come from?

502

De eso estoy pidiendo mi limosma.
    a. From that I am asking my alms.
    b. That is exactly what I desire.

De esto no hay todos los días.

ᔈ 503 ᔇ

De esto no hay todos los días.
    a. Of this there isn't everyday.
    b. Of this one does not partake everyday.

ᔈ 504

Después de atole.
    a. After the gruel.
    b. After the fact.
    c. It was done too late.

ᔈ 505 ᔇ

Dicho y hecho.
    a. Said and done.
    b. No sooner said than done.

ᔈ 506 ᔇ

Dió su brazo a torcer.
    a. He gave his arm to be twisted.
    b. He let them twist his arm.
    c. He let them have their way.
    d. He gave up.

ᔈ 507 ᔇ

El que tiene, tiene. (humorístico)
    a. The one who has, has.
    b. The person who possesses it has it.
    c. If you have it, you have it. (humorous)

ᔈ 508 ᔇ

Entre más habla, menos dice.
    The more he talks, the less he says.

Es el cuento de nunca acabar.
    a. It is a story that never ends.
    b. It is a situation with no end.

Ese tipo me pisa los callos.
    a. That fellow steps on my corns.
    b. That person irritates me.
    c. That person rubs me the wrong way.

Es harina de otro costal.
    a. That is flour from another sack.
    b. That is an entirely different matter.

Es la ley de la vida.
    a. It is the law of life.
    b. Such is life.

Esperé todo el santo día.
    a. I waited the whole holy day.
    b. I waited the whole blessed day.

Es plato de segunda mesa.
    a. It's a plate from a second table.
    b. He's her second choice.

515

Es su mero mole.
   a. It is his real mole. (Mole is a Mexican dish of turkey or
      chicken prepared with chile gravy.)
   b. That is his forte.

516

Está a todo dar.
   This is great.

517

Está como me la recetó el doctor.
   a. It's like the doctor prescribed it for me.
   b. It's exactly what the doctor ordered.

518

Está hablando por hablar.
   He is talking for the sake of talking.

519

Estamos viendo moros sin tranchetes.
   a. We are seeing Moors without knives.
   b. What we have before us is not a problem.
   c. We are magnifying the problem.

520

Están haciendo la perra.
   a. They are doing the female dog.
   b. They are loafing.

❧ 521 ❧

Está por las nubes.
a. It's by the clouds.
b. It's out of this world.
c. The price is sky high.

❧ 522 ❧

Está tan claro que hasta los ciegos lo ven.
a. It is so clear that even the blind can see it.
b. The answer is so obvious that anyone can see it.

❧ 523 ❧

Estiró la pata.
a. He stretched the leg.
b. He stretched his leg.
c. He passed away.

❧ 524 ❧

Estoy como el que chifló en la loma.
a. I'm like the one who whistled on the hill.
b. I was left excited and frustrated.

❧ 525 ❧

Estoy mojado hasta el tuétano.
a. I am soaked to the marrow.
b. I am soaked to the bone.

❧ 526 ❧

Es un caballero sin caballo.
a. He is a horseman without a horse.
b. He is a gentleman without a horse.
c. He is not a true gentleman.

∾ 527 ∾

Ganó la batalla pero perdió la guerra.
He won the battle but he lost the war.

∾ 528 ∾

Hablando del diablo.
a. Speaking of the devil.
b. Speak of the devil.
c. Here comes the person of whom we were speaking.

∾ 529 ∾

Hace su santa voluntad.
a. He does his holy desire.
b. He does whatever he wants to do.

∾ 530 ∾

La hicieron menos.
a. They made her less.
b. They slighted her.

∾ 531 ∾

Le gusta la mala vida.
He likes the bad life.

∾ 532 ∾

Le hice la barba.
a. I did his beard.
b. I shaved him.
c. I flattered him.

∾ 533 ∾

Les dieron rienda suelta.
a. They gave them a free rein.
b. They let them do as they please.

Llegó con los brazos cruzados.
    a. He arrived with his arms crossed.
    b. He arrived at the function with nothing to contribute.

Llueve a cántaros.
    a. It is raining jugs.
    b. It is raining cats and dogs.

Lo hizo en un dos por tres.
    a. He did it in a two by three.
    b. He did it very quickly.

¡Lo veo pero no lo creo!
    I see it, but I don't believe it!

Más claro ni el agua.
    a. More clear not even the water.
    b. It couldn't be more clear.

Me cayó como anillo al dedo.
    a. It fit me like a ring on the finger.
    b. This is exactly what I needed.

Me dejaron listo y alborotado.
    They left me ready and excited.

Me dejó plantada.
    a. He left me planted.
    b. He stood me up.
    c. He didn't come to see me as he promised.

Me doy por vencido.
    I give up.

Me hace los mandados. (humorístico)
    a. He does (runs) my errands. (humorous)
    b. He does what I tell him to do.
    c. I have him eating out of my hand.

Me sacó un pie por delante.
    a. He stuck out a foot in front of me.
    b. He got ahead of me.

Mete cinta para sacar listón.
    a. He puts in tape to take out a ribbon.
    b. He contributes a little to obtain a lot.

Me voy a dar una manita de gato.
    a. I'm going to give myself a little hand of a cat.
    b. I'm going to give my face a lick and a promise.
    c. I'm going to powder my nose.

⚘ 547 ⚘

Mira y calla.
   a. Look and be silent.
   b. Look but don't say anything,

⚘ 548 ⚘

No es cosa de otro mundo.
   a. It's not a thing from another world.
   b. That's not hard to believe.

⚘ 549 ⚘

No es santo de mi devoción.
   a. He is not a saint of my devotion.
   b. He's not my type.

⚘ 550 ⚘

No hay moros en la costa.
   a. There are no Moors on the coast.
   b. There are no obstacles in your way.

⚘ 551 ⚘

No le baila un frijol en la panza. (humorístico)
   a. A bean doesn't dance in his stomach. (humorous)
   b. He is living from hand to mouth.
   c. He has limited resources.

⚘ 552 ⚘

No me des cuerda.
   a. Don't wind my spring.
   b. Don't encourage me.

553

No me eches la sal.
   a. Do not throw salt on me.
   b. Do not bring me bad luck.

554

¡No qué no!
   So it wasn't going to happen!

555

No quiso dar su brazo a torcer.
   a. He did not want to give his arm to twist.
   b. He did not want to give in.

556

No sabe lo que es bueno.
   He/she does not know what is good.

557

No te hagas de boca chiquita.
   a. Don't pretend to have a small mouth.
   b. Take all you want.

558

No te quemes las pestañas.
   a. Do not burn the eyelashes.
   b. Don't burn the midnight oil.
   c. Do not study too hard tonight.

559

No vale la pena.
   It is not worth the effort.

≈ 560 ≈

No vale un comino.
   a. It is not worth a cumin seed.
   b. It is not worth a plugged nickel.

≈ 561 ≈

No vengo a ver si puedo sino porque puedo vengo.
   a. I do not come to see if I can, but I come because I can.
   b. I do not come to see if I can do the job; I come because I can do the job.

≈ 562 ≈

Pa' cuando tu vas, yo ya vine. (humorístico)
   By the time that you leave, I have arrived. (humorous)

≈ 563 ≈

Pa' luego es tarde.
   a. Later on is too late.
   b. Let's do it now.

≈ 564 ≈

Pa' que decirte que no, si sí.
   a. Why tell you no if yes.
   b. What's the use of telling you that it isn't so if it is so.

≈ 565 ≈

Pa' que decirte que sí, si no.
   a. Why tell you yes if no.
   b. What's the use of telling you that it is so if it isn't so.

≈ 566 ≈

Para el buen sueño no hay mala cama.
   a. For the good sleep, there is no bad bed.
   b. For the one who needs sleep, there is no bad bed.

ॐ 567 ॐ

Para el santo.
  a. For the saint.
  b. This small amount that you gave me is for my saint's day
     (birthday).
  c. This is not a big deal.

ॐ 568 ॐ

Para eso me pinto solo.
  a. For that I can paint myself.
  b. I can do that on my own.

ॐ 569 ॐ

Parece macho de viuda.
  a. He looks like a widow's man.
  b. He appears to be a man without a woman.

ॐ 570 ॐ

Pasé la noche de claro en claro.
  I didn't sleep a wink.

ॐ 571 ॐ

Poco más o menos.
  a. A little more or less.
  b. More or less.

ॐ 572 ॐ

Pregúntenme del milagro pero no me pregunten del santo.
  a. Ask me about the miracle but don't ask me about the
     saint.
  b. I'll tell you what happened but don't ask me who did it.

Que te vaya bien, que te vaya mal, que te pique un animal, en la orilla del canal. (humorístico)

May things go well, may things go badly, may an animal bite you at the edge of the canal. (Said humorously by one child to a child who is departing.)

∽ 574 ∾

Que tierno para despedirse.
a. How young to say good-bye.
b. He's immature at saying good-bye.
c. He left without saying good-bye.

∽ 575 ∾

¿Quién te dió vela en este entierro?
a. Who gave you a candle in this funeral?
b. Who invited you into this conversation?

∽ 576 ∾

Se encontró con la horma de su zapato.
a. He found his shoe's shoe tree.
b. He met someone just like himself.

∽ 577 ∾

Se hizo guaje.
a. He made a gourd of himself.
b. He pretended not to know.
c. He pretended not to understand.

∽ 578 ∾

Se hizo tonto.
a. He made himself the fool.
b. He pretended not to understand.

≈ 579 ≈

Se le pasó la mano.
    a. His hand went beyond.
    b. He went too far.

≈ 580 ≈

Se me hizo agua la boca.
    a. My mouth turned to water.
    b. It made my mouth water.

≈ 581 ≈

Se quedaron con el ojo cuadrado.
    a. They stayed with a squared eye.
    b. They were flabbergasted.

≈ 582 ≈

Se quedó bien picado.
    a. He remained stimulated.
    b. He remained unsatisfied.

≈ 583 ≈

Se salió con la suya.
    She got her own way.

≈ 584 ≈

Se tragó el cuento.
    a. He swallowed the story.
    b. He believed the tale he was told.
    c. He believed the falsehood.

≈ 585 ≈

Siempre corriendo y llegando tarde.
    a. Always running and arriving late.
    b. I'm always hurrying, but I still get there late.

～ 586 ～

Sin esfuerzo sale un verso.
    a. Without effort sprouts a verse.
    b. You said something poetic/clever without even trying.

～ 587 ～

Si no lo veo, no lo creo.
    a. If I don't see it, I don't believe it.
    b. I'm from Missouri, show me.

～ 588 ～

Son de camada.
    a. They are from the same litter.
    b. They are the same age.

～ 589 ～

Soy todo oídos.
    a. I am all ears.
    b. You have my full attention.

～ 590 ～

Su vida es un libro abierto.
    His life is an open book.

～ 591 ～

Te está tomando el pelo.
    a. He is taking your hair.
    b. He is making a fool of you.
    c. He is kidding you.

～ 592 ～

Vamos a echar una cana al aire.
    a. Let us throw a grey hair to the wind.
    b. Let's have a good time.

☙ 593 ☙

Vete con la música a otra parte.
a. Go someplace else with the music.
b. Go someplace else with your story.

☙ 594 ☙

Vete por la sombrita.
a. Go in the shade.
b. Walk in the shade.
c. Walk under the shade's protection.

☙ 595 ☙

Ya apareció el peine.
a. The comb has appeared.
b. The missing detail has been found.

☙ 596 ☙

Ya llegó por quien lloraban. (humorístico)
a. The one for whom weep has arrived. (Said humorously by a person who joins a gathering of people.)
b. Here I am. I have finally arrived.

Expresiones políticas
Polite Expressions

❧ 597 ❧

A los pies de usted.
   a. At your feet. (Said to a lady by a gentleman.)
   b. At your service.

❧ 598 ❧

Buen provecho.
   a. Good benefit.
   b. To your benefit.
   c. To your health.
   d. Enjoy.

❧ 599 ❧

Dichoso los ojos que te ven.
   a. Fortunate are the eyes that see you.
   b. How happy I am to see you.
   c. You are a sight for sore eyes.

❧ 600 ❧

Favor que usted me hace.
   a. A favor that you do for me.
   b. You're too kind.
   c. Don't mention it.

❧ 601 ❧

Muchos días de estos.
   a. Many of these days.
   b. May you have many of these days.
   c. Happy birthday.

❧ 602 ❧

Palabra de honor.
   a. Word of honor.
   b. On my word of honor.
   c. I give you my word.

❧ 603 ❧

Para servir a Dios y a usted.
   a. To serve you and God.
   b. At your service.
   c. I am here to serve you.
   d. I am at your service.

❧ 604 ❧

Pasó a mejor vida.
   a. He passed to a better life.
   b. He passed away.

❦ 605 ❧

Primero las damas.
   a. First the ladies.
   b. Ladies first.
   c. Let the ladies go first.

❦ 606 ❧

¡Qué aproveche!
   a. That you enjoy it!
   b. May you enjoy it!
   c. Enjoy it!
   d. Enjoy!

❦ 607 ❧

Que sueñes con los angelitos.
   a. May you dream with the little angels.
   b. Pleasant dreams.

❦ 608 ❧

Tus deseos son órdenes.
   a. Your wishes are orders.
   b. Your wish is my command.

Expresiones acerca de México y los mexicanos

Expressions About Mexico and Mexicans

～ 609 ～

Como México no hay dos.
- a. There are not two like Mexico.
- b. Like Mexico there is not another.
- c. There is only one Mexico.
- d. Mexico is unique.

～ 610 ～

Es más mexicano que el mole.
- a. He is more Mexican than mole. (Mole is a popular Mexican chile gravy which contains chicken or turkey.)
- b. He is as Mexican as they come.

Como México no hay dos.

⸎ 611 ⸎

Es mexicano hasta las cachas.
   a. He is Mexican to the handle.
   b. He is Mexican to the hilt.
   c. He is Mexican to the core.

⸎ 612 ⸎

Hasta que llovió en Cholula.
   a. Until it rained in Cholula (a city in Mexico).
   b. It finally happened.

Hasta que llovió en Cholula.

613

¡Jalisco, no te rajes!
   a. Jalisco, don't give up!
   b. Jalisco, don't back down!
   c. Jalisco (one of the Mexican states), keep trying.

614

México, cuida tu raza.
   a. Mexico, take care of your race.
   b. Mexico, take care of your people.
   c. Mexico, protect your population.

615

¡México de mis amores!
   a. Mexico of my loves!
   b. Mexico is my cherished love.

616

¡México, lindo y querido!
   a. Mexico, pretty and dearly loved!
   b. Mexico, you are great and I dearly love you!

617

Pobre de México—tan lejos de Dios y tan cerca a los Estados Unidos. (humorístico)
   Poor Mexico—so far from God and so close to the United States. (humorous)

618

¿Quién dice que no soy mexicano?
   a. Who says I am not Mexican?
   b. Who says I am not a true Mexican?

¿Quién dice que no soy mexicano?

References

The authors recommend the following references to those individuals interested in learning more about Mexico, the Spanish language, the Mexican culture, the Mexican American people, and American expressions as they relate to Spanish expressions.

Ballesteros, Octavio A. *Mexican Proverbs: The Philosophy, Wisdom and Humor of a People*. Austin, Texas: Eakin Press, 1979.

Ballesteros, Octavio A., and María del Carmen Ballesteros. *Mexican Sayings: The Treasure of a People*. Austin, Texas: Eakin Press, 1992.

Barker, Marie E. *Español Para el Bilingüe*. Skokie, Illinois: National Textbook Company, 1973.

Cassagne, J. M. *101 Spanish Idioms: Understanding Spanish Language and Culture Through Popular Phrases*. Lincolnwood, Illinois: Passport Books, 1996.

Celorio, Marta, and Annette C. Barlow. *Handbook of Spanish Idioms*. New York: Regents Publishing Company, 1973.

Galván, Roberto A. *The Dictionary of Chicano Spanish*. Lincolnwood, Illinois: NTC Publishing Group, 1996.

Girard, Alexander. *The Magic of a People*. New York: The Viking Press, 1968,

Nicholson, Irene. *The X in Mexico*. Garden City, New York: Doubleday and Company, 1966.

Pierson, Raymond H. *Guide to Spanish Idioms*. Lincolnwood, Illinois: Passport Books, 1996.

Samora, Julian, and Patricia V. Simon. *A History of the Mexican American People.* Notre Dame, Indiana: University of Notre Dame Press, 1993.

Savaiano, Eugene, and Lynn W. Winget. *Spanish Idioms.* Hauppauge, New York: Barron's Educational Series, Inc., 1996.

———. *2001 Spanish and English Idioms.* Hauppauge, New York: Barron's Educational Series, Inc., 1995.

Spears, Richard A. *Common American Phrases in Everyday Contexts.* Lincolnwood, Illinois: National Textbook Company, 1995.

Spears, Richard A. *NTC's American Idioms Dictionary.* Lincolnwood, Illinois: National Textbook Company, 1996.

Spears, Richard A., and Steven R. Kleinedler. *NTC's Dictionary of Everyday American English Expressions.* Lincolnwood, Illinois: NTC Publishing Group, 1996.

West, John O. *Mexican-American Folklore.* Little Rock, Arkansas: August House, 1988.

Wiener, Solomon. *Manual de Modismos Americanos Más Comunes.* New York: Regents Publishing Company, 1958.

About the Authors

OCTAVIO A. BALLESTEROS was born in San Antonio, Texas. He received his doctor of education degree from East Texas State University. His professional experiences include: (1) assistant professor of education at Sul Ross State University, (2) director of bilingual education/assistant professor of education at Incarnate Word College, (3) editor of *Catalyst for Change,* a national education journal, (4) assistant high school principal, (5) elementary school principal, (6) instructional coordinator at a large city jail, (7) instructional coordinator at a middle school, and (8) elementary bilingual education teacher. Ballesteros has taught twenty different courses at the university level. He presently teaches at the high school level for the San Antonio Independent School District. He is the author of six other books, including: *Mexican Proverbs: The philosophy, Wisdom and Humor of a People* (Austin, Texas: Eakin Press, 1979); *Mexican Sayings: The Treasure of a People* (Austin, Texas: Eakin Press, 1992); *Behind Jail Bars* (New York: Philosophical Library, 1979); and *Preparing Teachers for Bilingual Education: Basic Readings* (Washington, D.C.: University Press of America, 1979).

MARÍA DEL CARMEN BALLESTEROS was born in Mexico. She is a certified high school Spanish and art teacher. She also is certified to teach bilingual education at the elementary school level. She has taught Spanish and art at the high school level and art at the middle school level. The coauthor presently is a kindergarten bilingual teacher for the San Antonio Independent School District. She has a master of education degree from Our Lady of the Lake University and a bachelor of arts degree from Pan American University. The coauthor drew the fifteen illustrations in this book. María del Carmen Ballesteros is married to the author, Octavio A. Ballesteros. Octavio and María del Carmen live in the Monte Vista Historic District in San Antonio, Texas.